T0116971

Danger and Trust:

SAN QUENTIN, THE MEXICAN MAFIA AND THE CHICANO MOVEMENT

A Memoir

TED DAVIDSON

iUniverse, Inc.
New York   Bloomington

Danger and Trust: San Quentin, the Mexican
Mafia and the Chicano Movement

iUniverse books may be ordered through booksellers or by contacting:

iUniverse
1663 Liberty Drive
Bloomington, IN 47403
www.iuniverse.com
1-800-Authors (1-800-288-4677)

ISBN: 978-1-4502-0447-7 (pbk)
ISBN: 978-1-4502-0448-4 (ebook)

Printed in the United States of America

iUniverse rev. date: 3/01/2010

Contents

PREFACE

Danger and Trust: San Quentin, the Mexican Mafia and the Chicano Movement, is a Memoir I completed in 2009.

When I began my anthropological research among Chicano prisoners at San Quentin Prison in 1966, never in my wildest dreams did I imagine what frequently unforseen things would occur over the next 31 years—inside San Quentin for 20 months and then "on the streets" (outside of Prison) in California until 1997. Some of those unpredictable, almost incredible things included:

—Reaching the ultimate depths of the prisoners' own illegal and rule-breaking culture via the secretive—potentially deadly if crossed—Mexican Mafia.

—Being pulled into activities of the Chicano movement on the streets in California—thus expanding the scope of my research.

—Being angry and outraged that some of the staff members and administrators who are hired to manage the *ideal* prison system routinely ignore those ideals, mistreat the prisoners and hide their abusive acts from the public, including legislators.

—Being menacingly threatened by San Quentin administrators with prosecution by the Marin County District Attorney for revealing hidden staff secrets to the media; the Warden hoped my prosecution would lead to my being sent to prison with a number behind my name. Then, after strip searching me, angrily kicking me out of San Quentin.

—Being repeatedly set up by prison administrators or their representatives, to commit felonies—which I avoided.

—Giving shocking, revealing testimony to the California State Criminal Procedure Committee in Sacramento about facts that were hidden from the committee and other outsiders by prison administrators and California Department of Corrections (CDC).

—Discovering the true identity of under-cover agent-provocateurs who failed to provoke me to do things I would never have imagined doing, yet not revealing my discovery while I warily continued dealing with them; they never admitted their true identity to me.

—Being saddened and outraged—even though I understood the need for the FBI in our free society—that the FBI would attempt to set me up to commit felonies, destroy my livelihood, and ruin my family.

—Having officers of the Brown Berets and Black Panthers in my home in Berkeley.

—Being fired from Cabrillo College for daring to criticize California Department of Corrections and protesting the U.S. bombing of Cambodia.

—Writing a still-unique and still-largely-relevant, popular ethnography, *Chicano Prisoners: The Key to San Quentin,* that would remain in print for twenty-eight years.

—Living under a death threat against me, my wife and our two children for six weeks.

— Refusing to be pulled into becoming an advisor and writing for Edward James Olmos' 1992 movie, *American Me* which depicted some of the brutal reality faced by Chicano prisoners in prison— unfortunately one scene depicting the rape of a Mexican Mafia member was blatantly unrealistic; three advisors for the film were later murdered by the infuriated Mexican Mafia.

—Refusing to testify—thus avoiding the possibility of my being killed in retaliation by the Mexican Mafia—in a case against 12 Mexican Mafia members who were convicted in 1997 by the U.S. government of racketeering and conspiracy charges, including murder and extortion carried out in a bid to extend their influence beyond California prisons.

In this memoir I elaborate on the above-noted events and some of the many other things that occurred during the 31 years that I was involved with Chicano prisoners inside San Quentin Prison and with the Chicano movement on the streets in California.

The late 1960's and the following years were an exciting time in California, especially in Berkeley, and the San Francisco and Los Angeles areas: The Chicano movement. The Brown Berets. The so-called "race riots" at San Quentin. The Black Panthers. The Free Speech Movement at U.C. Berkeley. The *Berkeley Barb* underground newspaper. The Peace and Freedom Party. The war in Vietnam. Numerous manifestations of social protest in California during those years.

Chicano Prisoners: The Key to San Quentin is an ethnography which was published in 1974 and remained in print until 2004. Originally I wrote this book as R. Theodore Davidson, but since then I have used my less formal name, Ted Davidson, for works that I write.

Chicano Prisoners became a classic in ethnography, describing the salient features and hidden depths of the prisoners' own culture—very much as the prisoners themselves understand their largely illegal and/or rule-breaking culture.

My ethnography is truly unique in anthropology and penology. Almost the entire book has been included in two larger works—on Urban Anthropology and on Penology. My book helps the reader understand why prisoners think and act as they do in their culture and particularly gives considerable insight into the behavior of Chicano prisoners, and much more.

Parts of my ethnography are dated, but surprisingly **much** is the same—still being of value to those who *now* are interested in California prisons, Chicano prisoners, the birth and early development of the Mexican Mafia, types of prisoners, differences in behavior between Black and Chicano prisoners, failed efforts to apply anthropological knowledge to bring about legitimate change in our society, and much more.

When reading *Danger and Trust: San Quentin, the Mexican Mafia and the Chicano Movement*, readers who can find a used copy of my now out of print ethnography, *Chicano Prisoners: The Key to San Quentin*, will find it quite useful to read parts or all of the ethnography to enhance their knowledge about how I did my fieldwork for this longitudinal study of Chicanos—in prison and on the streets.

Personally, I understand the insidious, relentless spread of the increasingly violent Mexican Mafia from California prisons to many other parts of the United States. Unfortunately, the spread of the Mexican Mafia is a very real crisis in the making, recognized by authorities who are unable to stop it. Often Federal authorities unwittingly enhance the spread of the Mexican Mafia by convicting its members of Federal crimes and then sending them to Federal prisons in other states—across our nation.

Regrettably, I see no way to stop the spread of the Mexican Mafia which begins with peer pressure pushing quite young Chicanos to join local street gangs in the barrios, which often leads to membership in the Mexican Mafia and prison.

From their own perspective, members of the Mexican Mafia see themselves as successful in the way they have adapted to and are able to use the larger U.S. culture to their advantage.

Ted Davidson

How I started my research

In the fall of 1965, I entered the doctoral program in anthropology at the University of California, Berkeley. In the spring of 1966, Dr. Homer Hastings, Associate Warden, Care and Treatment at San Quentin Prison, approached Professor George Foster, my doctoral committee chairman, to see if he might know of a graduate student in anthropology who would be able to come over to San Quentin Prison for the summer as a work-study student and look into subcultural factors in the background of Mexican-American prisoners which made them excessively violent and excessively reluctant to participate in rehabilitation activities. Since my geographical area of specialty was Mexico and Meso-America, I was a natural choice for my professor.

Earlier, I had turned down a chance to apply for subvention funds from the University for the summer to support me while doing some short-term—somewhat pretend in my view—research which would be followed by a seminar paper in the fall. It seemed to be a far cry from the long-term, in-depth research anthropologists normally conducted. Consequently, since I had a wife and a one-year-old son to support, I had lined up a job to cut meat full-time for the summer; it paid much more than subvention funds.

However, when approached by my professor, I immediately realized the potential for turning the summer research at San Quentin Prison into my doctoral research. Even though the pay as a work-study student would be much less than cutting meat, I jumped at the chance to do what I considered *real* research. Also, it held potential for being much more significant than my earlier planned doctoral research in a Mexican peasant village—"Cognitive orientation & social change in rural Mexico."

In June 1966, I went to San Quentin Prison—as a work-study student, paid by U.C. Berkeley—to begin what initially was seen by prison administrators as a pilot project. But soon it turned into much more—my doctoral research. By the way, I was *not* locked up; I *did* go home at night.

Regardless of intense and at times frightening events, I feel fortunate to have been involved as a young anthropologist and to have come to understand those exciting times.

Please note: I do not use the term "Mexican-American" in this memoir. Soon after I began my research, the term "Chicano" came to be commonly used as a self-chosen term of address among Mexican-American prisoners. My use of "Chicano" is similar to my use of "Black" as the self-chosen term of address among Negro prisoners at that time. Also, I use the term "prisoner" as an adjective rather than having to continually use "prisoners" throughout this memoir. Therefore, using prisoner as an adjective, I refer to a variety of prisoner things, such as the prisoner perspective or the prisoner culture.

Also, let me clarify some terminology for the reader. At the much earlier change from California Department of *Prisons* to the more euphemistic-sounding California Department of *Corrections* (CDC), other terminology was changed. Now there are three divisions of staff in each prison as well as in CDC offices in Sacramento: Administration, Care and Treatment, and Custody. So, at San Quentin there are: Associate Warden Administration, Associate Warden Care and Treatment, and Associate Warden Custody. The Warden is similar to a CEO, on the top, above the Associate Wardens. It is important to note that Associate Warden *Custody* actually would be more appropriately named Associate Warden *Guards*. However the euphemism is used to de-emphasize the term. This is much like the current use of "Correctional Officer" for *guard* and "Inmate" for *prisoner*. There are only two "*prisons*" in California—Folsom and San Quentin. All the other prisons are euphemistically called things such as "Correctional Institutions."

MY FREEDOM AND CONSTRAINTS

I made it entirely clear and it was understood by prison administrators that it would be necessary for me—as an anthropologist, without condemning—to view the prison in a holistic manner, as a complete world, treating the complex, largely covert, yet quite real totality that the prisoners perceive, experience and know. This was a view of the prisoners and their largely illegal and rule-breaking culture that had not been revealed to outsiders before. I recognized—and many of the prisoners did too—that this view would fill an existing void and prove quite useful to students, professionals, lawmakers, and the general public. Consequently, I was given total freedom of movement throughout the prison—except for Death Row—by prison administrators.

Realizing the delicate nature of the type of information I would probably encounter if I were to accomplish my task, prison administrators agreed that I would *not* have to reveal any confidential information to the staff. The two exceptions would have been if I had learned that someone was going to be physically harmed or that the prisoners were going to destroy the prison in some manner.

Scientists and others had studied prisoners in San Quentin before and had taken advantage of the offers made by staff. Those routine staff offers were extended to me. I could use an office in the custody and staff office area inside the prison walls. Also, I was given a list of Chicano prisoners who would be amenable to talking to me. In addition, I would be allowed to use the "ducat" system—I could fill out a list of prisoners, and they would receive ducats to appear at my office (or in a classroom in the education building if several prisoners were meeting with me) at the time I had indicated.

I surprised the administrator who made the offer by declining their standard offers, indicating I would prefer to go to where the prisoners normally were rather than have them ordered to see me in the confines of a small office or a classroom. As I've often said, regardless of where I was in the prison, my shoes were my office.

Always clean shaven and dressed in a suit and tie to avoid being thwarted by the staff, I went to where the prisoners were during their daily activities (such as in their cells and at their jobs). My frequently being seen by guards in places where free men seldom or never went alone aroused curiosity—occasionally bordering on hostility. Some of the guards thought I was a counselor, from the way I was dressed. However, they were puzzled and suspicious of the fact that I would often be in places that a counselor would never be—isolated with one or more prisoners, out of sight and/or sound of any guards or other staff members. Gradually more guards and other staff members learned who I was and what I was doing at San Quentin.

Initially I had been advised to approach and introduce myself and explain my presence to any staff member (such as a guard or work supervisor) when going into an area for the first time. This turned out to be an excellent way to learn things from non-prisoners. Gradually my self-introduction became unnecessary as more staff came to know, through their grapevine, who I was.

A particular incident is interesting as an illustration of what I could learn from first-encounter conversations. One day I was going to the industries area. There is a single entrance into that walled area where prisoner movement in and out of the industries area is controlled by a single guard in a tiny shack next to the single opening in the wall. Not recognizing the guard, I stopped, introduced myself and explained my presence. Soon, the guard began expounding about how the Chicanos were a sub-species of the human race! I couldn't believe what I was hearing. I bit my tongue! The challenge (as an anthropologist who wanted to learn what the "natives" thought) was to look interested and not visibly react or vehemently argue with the guard. This was a tremendous challenge to me, because on the streets I would have forcefully argued with someone who said such things.

Later I reflected on the incident. I assumed that normally, the guard would abide by his duties and enforce the routine the prisoners were supposed to follow. However, I wondered how he would react in a riotous situation—such as the *so-called* race riots of 1967 at San

Quentin. Would he have been one of the guards who manipulated and abused the prisoners? (I will treat those race riots in considerable detail later.)

My initial interaction with prisoners was different than that with staff. At the beginning of my research, after introducing myself to and interacting with a of couple Chicano prisoners—satisfying their curiosity about me—I often would be personally introduced to another prisoner or be told, "Talk with my buddy. I already told him about you." Consequently, during the beginning of my research I often would have a personal introduction from one prisoner to the next. At that time, almost all of the prisoners I talked with were Chicanos.

My venturing to places where free men seldom if ever ventured and talking with one or a few prisoners in depth struck them as being decidedly different. The prisoners were extremely interested in who *I* was—this guy in a suit and tie who'd show up in the most unlikely places for a free man to be.

At the start, I was disappointed that I learned so little from those early conversations. However, I soon realized why *they* asked most of the questions and why *I* did most of the talking and explaining. The Chicano prisoners wanted to allay their suspicions about me—not wanting to reveal important things to an outsider who might betray them or use confidential information against them. Their curiosity and extreme interest about who I was and what I was doing there soon paid off. When talking with them, after first stating the thrust of why I was there as a work-study student, I *confidentially* shared what I intended to do in addition to the summer pilot project. I told them that I was going to stay beyond the summer to learn as much as possible about *their* culture inside, and ultimately to write a book to "tell it like it is." They agreed with what I was trying to accomplish—stressing that no one had ever really told it like it is, not as the prisoners themselves see and perceive *their* world inside prison. My long-term intentions apparently were quickly shared with other prisoners. After a short time the volume of questions to me diminished—since an increasing number of prisoners learned about me through their many contacts with other prisoners. Soon, many prisoners I had never met knew a great deal about me. Our conversations became more relaxed—a mutual sharing and learning experience. To them, our conversations or discussions were strikingly different from any *"interview"* they had engaged in with researchers in the past.

A critical tool used by anthropologists in their research is participant observation. At times it may be possible for an anthropologist to almost totally immerse himself or herself in a culture—virtually becoming a native of that culture. However, in most research situations, there are reasonable, appropriate limits on how much the anthropologist participates and observes. Inside San Quentin I was limited in many respects to the degree that I could participate and observe—limits placed by prison administrators and staff, by prisoners and by myself. As for me, the last thing I wanted to do was to break some law and be convicted of a crime. (After being kicked out of San Quentin, I repeatedly evaded illegal attempts and enticements by authorities and undercover agents to get me to commit felonies so they could—as Warden Nelson hopefully said, "Get him in prison with a number behind his name!" *Some* of their failed efforts will be treated later.)

Surprisingly however, with my freedom of movement and access to most prisoners for private and/or small group conversations, and to many of their activities (both legal and illegal), I was able to gain a wealth of information.

Numerous times my relationship with prisoners I had met inside continued on the streets, when they would be paroled and visit me in my home in Berkeley. Seeing me, my wife and two small children living in a small, rustic cottage in the Berkeley hills confirmed their feelings about me—that I was for real. This additional evaluation and confirmation of my honesty and sincerity repeatedly made its way back to prisoners still in prison where I continued my research.

Owing to the persistent suspicion and paranoia among many if not most prisoners and guards at the beginning of my research, I purposely took no notes while at the prison. Had I taken notes, many of the prisoners would never have talked to me, and numerous staff members would have been very guarded when talking with me—possibly suspicious that I was spying on them and/or the prison system.

Not taking notes was a tremendous challenge. Had someone told me before I began my research that I could not take notes at the prison, I wouldn't have thought it would be possible. However, I forced myself to try to remember every thing that happened each day. At home in the evening, I would sit down at my typewriter and type notes as I tried to re-live and remember as much as possible. Soon I became adept at remembering almost all that happened earlier that day. It was demanding—having to recall and re-think what happened. It took nearly as long to do my notes as it did to live through the original experiences. If personal or family obligations precluded typing the notes the first evening, the next evening I would only be able to remember about half of what had occurred the previous day. If another evening passed, by the third evening I would have forgotten almost everything. With time, I was able to type about 10 to 12 pages of field notes each night.

An unanticipated reward occurred from typing notes each evening. The process of re-living the events of the day and putting them on paper effectively transferred those events from my short-term to my long-term memory. If someone had read those notes, the notes would have been interesting, but of limited value. However, to me, then, and even years later, when I read the notes it was like turning on a video camera. It had been impossible to relate all the details when typing, but my notes triggered sights, sounds and a wealth of things beyond the mere words in my notes.

(Let me briefly jump ahead to explain something quite important. Unfortunately, since 1989 I have never had access to the roughly 2,000 pages of typewritten field notes that I had earlier generated, and I probably never will see them again. So what I *now and henceforth* relate in this memoir are from memory and a random collection of assorted papers. In 1989 I filed for divorce and moved out within a few months. I took a load of my things in my van to a cottage I had rented. When I returned a few hours later, my key would not work. My wife had the locks changed. I never was able to get into my home again to retrieve anything else—including my notes and a wide assortment of other notes and papers. In spite of that, things cannot be changed. But there is one reason why I now have no regrets about the time I spent re-living events that I experienced inside San Quentin and typing my field notes. That often demanding earlier activity has now proven to be a useful boon for my long-term memory.)

Logically, owing to the subcultural factors in the background of Chicano prisoners that I intended to research as a work-study student, the first prisoners I talked with were Chicanos. I had been told by administrators and many staff members that the Chicanos were the most difficult group to crack—most of them would not snitch and were very closed about revealing things to staff or outsiders. *That* was why administrators wanted me to do the research in the first place.

Without realizing it, I was quite fortunate to have all of my initial research be with Chicanos. Initially putting most of my efforts into establishing rapport with them significantly precluded my dealing with Black and Anglo prisoners. After I entered into the confidence of Chicanos and they trusted and felt very comfortable with me, I had time for and was able to deal with Black and Anglo prisoners too. Later I was told by Chicano convicts and by a member of the Mexican Mafia that *if* I had begun my research with Black prisoners (who generally are regarded as potential snitches by convicts), I would have failed—that a barrier would have precluded Chicano prisoners, and especially members of the Mexican Mafia, from ever talking with me and revealing the depths of the prisoner culture to me.

Let me take an important, necessary aside at this point regarding my use of the terms *prisoners, convicts* and *inmates* in this memoir. A full treatment of these three terms can be found in my book, *Chicano Prisoners: The Key to San Quentin*, Holt, Rinehart and Winston, Inc., 1974. This still-unique ethnography was in print until 2002. Admittedly, numerous things have changed over 33 years. However, many of the things depicted in this still-relevant, still-unique book continue to be true. In *Chicano Prisoners* I carefully differentiate between prisoners, convicts and inmates. I readily admit that some of the noted differences between convicts and inmates *may no longer be as valid today as they were over 30 years ago*, so please recognize this—I certainly do.

Many years ago, when the California Department of *Prisons* was changed to Department of *Corrections*, staff dropped the term prisoners and replaced it with inmates. The terms convict and prisoner were seldom used by staff after that change from a *prison* system to a *correctional* system

However, some prisoners—convicts—make a distinction between two *types* of prisoners: convicts and inmates. But, most prisoners—who also are the majority of inmates—are not aware of the differences between the two types. Convicts, who routinely use the terms convicts and inmates to differentiate two *types* of prisoners, are not confused that the term inmates also can refer to *all* prisoners. The context of their conversations easily reveals the meaning to them. To aid readers of my works and avoid repeated unnecessary qualification, I have taken the liberty of replacing one of the uses of inmates with prisoners—referring to *all* prisoners.

Convicts live by the convict code. Ideally, they *never* snitch and never do something for their personal benefit that would be detrimental to the group or another member of the group. In reality though, convicts *almost never* snitch; but if one should and be caught, he probably would be executed in accord with the convict code.

An inmate, concerned only for himself, has no sense of duty toward, unity with, or real concern for other prisoners. Inmates may report to staff on the illegal and rule-breaking activities of convicts, so convicts understandably think of inmates as rats, snitches and punks. When inmates are busted by staff, they usually will inform on any and every possible person to try to get out of a tight situation. Since inmate snitches do not come under the authority of the convict code, they would not be executed, but would be ostracized. Inmates are the enemy, and convicts must take care to hide their important illegal and rule-breaking activities from them. I will follow the lead of convicts and use their meanings.

Please note well. It was impossible for me to view the prisoner culture with total objectivity. Those who would make such a claim have never been involved enough to be allowed to fathom the ultimate depths of that culture. As a participant observer, I came to know many prisoners well; some of them came to be my close friends. They openly and generously shared their thoughts, experiences, and emotions with me. Consequently, I was able to observe, sense, feel, and know the reality of the prisoner culture—often with considerable emotion.

I recognize that the prisoner perspective is subject to biases, and my use of this perspective exposed my research to those biases. However,

I simultaneously attempted to temper my necessary involvement with the detachment of an outsider and anthropologist. Hopefully, I was able to avoid the excessive ethnocentrism of some prisoners and present the prisoners world in a cultural relativistic manner. It should be stressed that the outsiders' perspective (the one which usually is used by those who write about prisoners) also is subject to biases—a different set of biases. In addition, the outsiders' perspective is relatively far removed from the vast amount of activity that covertly takes place within the prisoner culture.

Had I not become involved as I did, I could never have comprehended the real prisoner culture and presented it as a culture that still is unique among existing ethnographies. I believe that if we are searching for the reality of a culture, for as true a picture as possible, we must endeavor to see, sense, and feel that culture as its members do. I maintain that it was necessary and fruitful to do as I did. The resultant knowledge, emotions, feelings, and biases were the necessary foundation of my research. I believe my application of a degree of objectivity enabled me to write *Chicano Prisoners*, an ethnography that comes as close as possible to the true reality of the prisoner culture.

First Months

My first week at San Quentin in June of 1966 entailed taking orientation with four new guards. Administrators thought it would be the easiest way to introduce me to the prison and much of the routine. That way they would not have to have a guard personally lead me around for a private orientation. I did everything the new guards did except go to the firing range. I learned a lot about where things were located and much of the *legal* routine. Also, I met most of the administrators and higher-ranking guards. Prisoners who saw me with the new guards who were being oriented probably assumed I too was a new guard.

After orientation, as my rapport with Chicano prisoners became well-established and I felt comfortable going to almost any place in the prison, I ended up occasionally doing somewhat unconventional things for a free man to do, in places where a free man seldom if ever went.

The staff gradually became accustomed to my occasionally unusual behavior. Prisoners did the same, and soon allowed me to observe rule-breaking or illegal activities that—if they had been caught—possibly would have led to disciplinary actions.

BRUNCH

One example is the time I had brunch with a prisoner in his cell. West Block is the honor block at San Quentin. Here, for the prisoners who have a positive behavior record inside and have earned the privilege of living in the West Block, the rules are quite lax. They are free to move in and out of their cells during the day and evening. They can watch TV, work out in the West Block exercise yard, go to different areas of the prison, attend classes or meetings of various groups and numerous other things. Compared to the South, East and North Blocks, the prisoners in West Block have relatively few constraints on their daytime and evening activities. A single guard normally sits in the small guard office on the ground floor, seldom climbing the stairs to go up on the tiers.

One morning I dropped by prisoner A's cell to talk with him as we had several times before in other places in the prison. He and prisoner B were in A's cell, on the lower bunk bed, leaning back against the cement wall on one side, with their feet against the opposite wall—4 ½ feet away—talking and having some coffee. Prisoner A immediately invited me in to join their conversation and soon whispered something to the prisoner B, who temporarily excused himself and left. Soon prisoner B returned to the cell with a cup of coffee for me and sweet rolls for the three of us. We continued our conversation as prisoner B hopped up on the upper bunk and sat with his feet dangling over the side. I soon had my back and feet against opposite walls. We enjoyed our brunch as we continued our friendly conversation.

What was involved in our brunch? If a prisoner had play money from his inmate account, he could purchase the instant coffee in the canteen. Thus, having the *coffee* was not breaking any rules. The very hot water was piped throughout the prison. The "cup" for the coffee was a large (about 12 ounce) thick plastic glass, wrapped with black electrical tape for insulation. However, possession of the sweet rolls broke some rules—grounds for minor disciplinary sanctions, which would not be enforced in the West Block. The sweet rolls had probably been made in the prison bakery early that morning and smuggled out (against the rules) after some prisoner had breakfast. Then prisoner A bought the sweet rolls from the smuggler-prisoner who (against the rules) probably was running a small store from his cell. All of this was quite insignificant compared to some of the illegal and rule-breaking activities of prisoners inside the prison.

PAROLE HEARINGS

Soon after beginning my research, a prison administrator suggested I visit a few parole hearings. The parole board is called Adult Authority in California. I did as he suggested.

The Adult Authority (also called "the board") conducts hearings for prisoners who are legally eligible for parole. Two board members hold hearings for several days at one prison and then go to another prison. The board determines which prisoners who are eligible for parole will be given a parole date and which will be made to wait another year or more. With many hearings and limited time, about 10 to 15 minutes are allowed for each prisoner. While one member questions prisoner A, the other member is busy skimming the "jacket" (record file) of prisoner B, the next prisoner to be heard—and simultaneously half-listens to the current interview. After prisoner A leaves, the members discuss the case and make their decision, being ready for prisoner B within 3 to 5 minutes. When prisoner B comes in, the member who had skimmed B's jacket conducts the hearing while the other member skims the next prisoner's jacket (prisoner C's) and half-listens. Members repeat this alternating routine day by day; it becomes quite perfunctory.

As a silent observer, I attended the board hearing of a Chicano prisoner who was questioned by the board representative who had skimmed his jacket during the previous hearing. After several rather perfunctory questions, the board member asked about the crime for which the prisoner had been convicted. Then, some pointed questions about the activities of his alleged crime partner who had not been convicted made the prisoner very uncomfortable. He tried to avoid answering, but the questions were asked again. Facing the board representative who embodied the potential for freedom, the prisoner, with visible emotion showing in his face, told an obvious lie, refusing to snitch on his alleged crime partner.

After the prisoner left the room, the representatives laughed and noted, to me, that it was an example of how the "Mexican-Americans will never rat on anyone." I found it difficult to believe what I was hearing. They had no valid reason to question the prisoner about his alleged crime partner. In court, the prisoner had refused to inform on his crime partner and was serving a sentence that took that into consideration. To me, it appeared that they did this merely as an amusing example. They obviously had no compassion for the prisoner and no understanding of the conflict situation in which they placed him as a fellow human being. They forced him to tell them an obvious lie when they held his freedom in their hands. I was shocked—these were men who had been hired for their ability to understand the situations faced by other human beings.

Another example of a board hearing involved a prisoner who was returned to prison for violating his parole by writing a bad check four months after his release. The board representative verbally reviewed what had taken place two years earlier, and the prisoner murmured the expected agreement. The representative pointed out that the prisoner was let out on parole to a job, but was fired in about two weeks. Then the prisoner found and soon lost another job. Before long another job was followed by getting fired. Finally, after about three or four weeks, the prisoner wrote a bad check.

The board member pointed out how stupid that was. He went on with his lecture, noting that the prisoner should have lined himself up with one of the many small loan companies out there—for a small loan to tide him over until he got himself lined up with a steady job. Hiding his true feelings of astonishment, the prisoner merely muttered agreement. Fortunately the prisoner's submissive performance was worthwhile and successful. The board member told the prisoner that— since he had served two years for the parole violation and now saw his error—he was again ready for parole.

I couldn't believe the gross ignorance the representative demonstrated—ignorance of the larger world in which the prisoner must live when he is released on parole. I doubted that there was a loan company in existence that would have knowingly lent the parolee money under those circumstances. And, no parole agent working for CDC would have given the parolee approval to sign such a loan contract.

I have *never* been able to forget those hearings and *how I felt and still feel.* As an observer, I was not allowed to say a word. Other than me, the two board representatives and one prisoner at a time, the only additional person in attendance was a San Quentin counselor who silently took some brief notes that would be put into the prisoner's jacket (record file). After attending board hearings two times, I was disgusted by what I thought were extremely sad and unfair proceedings. Also, I was embarrassed by even being there as an observer, and by having to remain silent and not reveal my feelings while watching the prisoners endure the hearings, which frequently were agonizing for them.

Since I am on the subject of parole hearings, let me share another experience that occurred much later. A Chicano convict, ND, who later became a good friend, worked in one of several maintenance shops in what was called "the alley," where we had long conversations. One day, when I dropped by to talk with him, he seemed quite depressed. In response to my asking what was the matter, he indicated that he had a letter from his wife in which she indicated she was going to stop visiting him! This was quite a blow, for she had routinely visited him all the time he had been in San Quentin—often bringing their children too on the relatively long drive from their home in a town in the central valley of California.

Apparently his wife was upset by ND's indication to her of the reason given to him for the Adult Authority's most recent denial of his parole. She claimed that he must be lying to her, that there must be some *other* reason that he was hiding from her, because none of the reasons given in the past had ever seemed to make sense to her. Actually, the reasons had never made sense to ND either.

ND was serving time for dealing narcotics in his home town. There had been such strong local feeling about ND's crime that his wife was fired from her teaching position in the local school system, and was blackballed from teaching in the local school district. She was supporting herself and their children by working in a low-paying job that was far below her educational training and experience.

In order for me to make sense of the rest of this example for readers, it is important to briefly explain the indeterminate sentence law in California and how the Adult Authority administers it.

When the Department of *Corrections* was established to replace the Department of *Penology* in 1944, a new emphasis was placed on the 'correction' and 'rehabilitation' of prisoners—*not punishment*. The Adult Authority, replaced the old parole board. Under California's new indeterminate sentence law, the judge who sentences a convicted adult felon to prison no longer sets the term or duration of imprisonment. Certain felonies carry a mandatory life sentence. For other felony convictions, a minimum and maximum term of imprisonment is fixed by statute. Ideally, within those legal limits, the Adult Authority supposedly is to administer certain parts of the indeterminate sentence in a more scientific manner than the old parole board was able to do. Within those limits, the Adult Authority has the power to determine the total time a prisoner is to serve in prison and on parole—based on *when the prisoner becomes rehabilitated*. For example, a prisoner usually becomes eligible for parole after serving one third of his sentence in prison. If he is rehabilitated, he may be paroled from prison when eligible; but he must serve the remainder of his minimum sentence on parole. If successful on parole, he is discharged from CDC's authority when he completes his minimum sentence. But, if he does not become rehabilitated, he can be kept in prison until he has served his maximum sentence—to protect society and to punish him as a non-rehabilitated prisoner. When the maximum is reached, he must be discharged. However, if he should become rehabilitated at some point between the minimum and maximum, he is to be paroled at that time and discharged after successfully serving about two years on parole.

Ideally, California's indeterminate sentencing system is intended to protect society, while being humane and fair to prisoners. The Adult Authority is supposed to tailor the amount of correction and/or punishment each prisoner receives according to the individual needs deemed necessary for each prisoner. Unfortunately, these underlying ideals will never be achieved under the existing system because there is a basic defect in the way that the indeterminate sentence is administered—*there is absolutely no way to judge if a prisoner has become rehabilitated or not.*

With the cooperation of CDC, the Adult Authority has been able to effectively sidestep this defect. In lieu of admitting the impossibility of determining when and if a prisoner is rehabilitated, the Adult Authority has used its quasi-judicial and administrative power to set up a system that ignores many of the ideals that supposedly underlie California's indeterminate sentencing system.

In the ideally functioning system, it is evident that the key factor is the point in time *when the prisoner becomes rehabilitated.* Unfortunately, the system, in practice, stands in bitter contrast to the theoretical system. The Adult Authority—subject to pressures from outside the prison system—has taken a cautious approach to granting paroles. By making most prisoners spend from just under, to well over their minimum sentence in prison, it appears that the board has generally been able to avoid being criticized by the general public for being too lenient.

Back to ND's experience. ND had served somewhat more than the Adult Authority-established minimum time for his particular crime. *And* from the beginning of his time in prison he had been an exemplary prisoner. Each time he met with the board for parole consideration he had been turned down and the board advised him—always something different—what he should do to better his chances for getting parole next time, such as more group counseling, or more religion. He followed their advice, but it never made any difference at the following hearing.

ND had long-suspected there must be something involved in his repeatedly being turned down other than the rather meaningless reasons the board claimed, but he had no way of proving it. His suspicion, coupled with his wife's decision to no longer visit him pushed him into his current depression. I compassionately listened and expressed my understanding—and anger— at his situation. He recognized that I was unable to do anything to help other than listen as a friend.

Having thought about ND's situation, the next day I went to the administration building and read ND's jacket. The very brief notes made by the counselor-observer from ND's recent parole hearing were there, and the reason the board told him for his being denied was what ND had told me and what he had conveyed to his wife.

However, right below those notes were several recent *protest-panic letters* from members of ND's home town! Looking deeper into the file, I discovered that every year—before ND's parole hearing, similar letters had been written. Those letters to the Adult Authority expressed profound fear that, since ND was one of the worst criminals to have lived in their community, to release him so prematurely would be a dangerous mistake.

I did a great deal of thinking about what I possibly could do to help ND in some way. One of my greatest concerns had to do with the way that prison administrators and CDC control information from inside the prison. I knew that outsiders who volunteer their time to work with prisoners in a variety of ways are beholden to the prison administrators for entry into the prison and would be denied entry if they publicly criticize the prison system. *This would apply to me and my research.*

Even though it was risky for me to call ND's wife and potentially risk my research inside prison being terminated, my concern for ND and his family prevailed. That evening I called ND's wife from my home in Berkeley. It must have been a strange call for her to receive, but she listened. After carefully introducing myself, I explained that what I was doing was for her, ND and their children. I told her what I had learned about the board's refusal to grant ND parole, the so-called reason they gave, and the many negative letters from members of her community. I also told her that I had *not* discussed my making this call with ND, but that I merely was making the call as a friend who sympathized with ND's situation and depression. I wanted her to know the *real* story behind the recent refusal by the board—and possibly resume her visits. I could tell by her voice that she was in tears when we closed our conversation.

A few days later, I saw ND again. He greeted me with a smile and exclaimed that he had received a letter from his wife—saying that *someone* called her and explained the *real* reason why he was not being paroled—*protest-panic letters* from their home town. She would be making her routine visits again. Then, almost whispering, he asked if I had called her. My smile answered his question.

The next time I saw ND—the first time since the brief hiatus in his wife's visits—he indicated that when his wife visited over the weekend, she told him that she had received a call from a prison staff member who apparently had covertly read her letter before it was delivered to ND. The staff caller demanded that she reveal *who* made the phone call to her. She refused, *claiming* that the person never identified himself. The staff member snapped back that he didn't believe her and that it would negatively reflect on her husband if she didn't tell him. She still refused, so that ended their conversation.

ND and I discussed what had occurred and what I had done on his behalf. He was extremely grateful—for himself as well as his wife and their children. He assured me, that as a good *Chicana*, his wife would never snitch and reveal my identity; I knew that. Also, we bitterly shared the way that the Adult Authority avoids criticism from the public by abusing the indeterminate sentencing system and its basic defect—*not being able to judge if a prisoner has become rehabilitated or not.*

Prisoner Jackets

Another suggestion by an administrator was that I could read the jacket (record file) of any of the prisoners, thus enabling me to learn a great deal about prisoners I would deal with. Because I was so busy with other things that were more important to me at the beginning of my research, it was some time before I followed the administrator's suggestion.

I had been impressed and intrigued by CG. He was one of the prisoners I had extensively talked with. CG seemed to always have something insightful to say about almost any subject. I personally thought he was the brightest, most articulate prisoner I had yet to encounter. Being so favorably impressed, I looked at his jacket to learn more about him. Beyond the details about the crime he had committed, where he had lived and the like, the thing I was most interested in was his educational background.

What a shock! The intelligence testing he had undergone in one of CDC's two reception centers had concluded CG had *low to average intelligence*. I couldn't believe it! I checked to be certain that I had CG's jacket. It was his. However, the CG I knew was *brilliant*! I soon learned the reason for this gross discrepancy. Prisoners had quite negative feelings about CDC's two reception centers.

After being arrested, jailed, and convicted of committing a felony, a man who is sentenced to CDC for the first time begins serving his sentence with a four-to-eight-week stay in one of CDC's two reception-guidance centers. These centers test the physical, psychological, and social characteristics of men as they enter CDC. Many prisoners, staff members and counselors in particular, question the validity and benefit of much of this testing—which is never repeated, regardless of how long a man stays in prison. Nevertheless, this testing becomes the basic foundation of a man's permanent "jacket" and influences decisions regarding the man—even if the decisions are made many years after the testing. The reception-guidance centers are inside and are a relatively-isolated part of the prisons at Chino and Vacaville. But, the real shock of entering prison usually does not hit the prisoners then, because these centers are not like the regular prisons. At the centers, the feelings of prisoners are very different than those among prisoners when they enter a *real* prison such as San Quentin as a "fish" (new arrival). The major function of these centers is testing, and prisoners feel that the center staff are more considerate than those at the regular prisons. Prisoners note that even the guards at the centers tend to have a more tolerant attitude than guards in most CDC prisons. In addition, *all* the prisoners are fish, so none are in a position to take advantage of the situation or other fish.

Let me add to the above description. A new prisoner, before finding himself in prison, has recently gone through what he might consider hell: arrest, jail, possibly a trial, and perhaps several other onerous things along the way. Now, in the reception center, he is expected to cooperate with those who would test, evaluate and imprison him. Many new prisoners are understandably angry, belligerent and uncooperative. Consequently, they think there is no reason why they should bother about anything like tests. CG agreed with what I had learned about reception centers. He had purposely screwed up the tests—out of spite.

So, my *personal* evaluation of CG had not been changed by reading his jacket. And, after sampling the jackets of a couple other prisoners I had come to know fairly well, I concluded that I did not want to waste any more of my time reading jackets. I would greatly prefer to make my own evaluation of individual prisoners.

I'd like to add, later, when I was preparing to write *Chicano Prisoners*, I picked through my typewritten notes and pulled out *all* those I had made pertaining to CG. The stack of his ideas were so insightful, significant and useful that I routinely used them while writing my book.

WORK SUPERVISOR

When I was talking with a Chicano prisoner about his prison job on the all-Chicano inside construction team, he mentioned his Anglo free man work supervisor and made several very positive comments about him. The team liked the supervisor, who was very different from most work supervisors. They felt he was probably one of very few work supervisors who got along well with Chicanos. They would "work their butts off for him."

Soon I met the very genial, relaxed supervisor and privately talked with him. Unlike many other work supervisors, he had a significant understanding of Chicanos and a deep respect for his all-Chicano crew. He related several things to me, such as how he had learned to *ask* their opinion about a task, not *tell* them what to do or *order* them to do it. In praise, he proudly related how his crew had moved a huge number of cubic yards of dirt, by shovels, in a short period of time, in a past emergency.

DINNER GUEST INSIDE

Among the first Chicano prisoners I talked with at San Quentin was DD. I soon discovered he was an atypical Chicano. His father had been a labor contractor for Mexican-American migrant workers, leading to a very different upbringing for DD than most barrio Chicanos. DD recognized that he had usually been an outsider among Chicanos; he openly admitted that he really didn't know much about barrio life. I guessed that may have been why he had joined the very small Jewish religious group at San Quentin—which was indeed an unusual choice for someone raised in a predominantly Catholic subculture.

After a few months, in early September 1966, DD invited my wife and me to a special annual dinner and talent show, sponsored by the Jewish religious group and produced and presented by the prisoners.

The dinner and show were held in the south mess hall which was the newest and most attractive mess hall, with a huge (about 100-feet-long), very impressive mural depicting California's history—painted by a Chicano prisoner. A crew of prisoners had set up a stage, with props and special lighting and sound. Unlike the dingy *north* mess hall—where prisoners ate on long, stationary tables, and viewed weekend movies, but where the warden's tour *never* went—the *south* mess hall was comparatively cheerful with its 4-person, square café-sized tables with attached seats.

My wife did not want to miss the extremely rare chance to see inside the walls of the prison, even though she very obviously was pregnant with our second child. She was due to deliver within less than two weeks; so it made her appearance quite noticeable to the prisoners. We sat at one of the tables with two prisoners, DD and CW.

CW had been on the crew who had set up the lights for the show, so he was able to finagle his way into staying for the dinner and show. DD, CW, my wife and I sat at one of the small tables and soon were engaged in conversation while we ate and enjoyed the talent show. CW was pleasant and sociable with a ready smile, unlike DD who seemed somewhat reserved.

One brief memorable part of our pleasant conversation that evening involved my wife's quite obvious condition. All of us joked about how she looked like she was going to have twins. When we left, CW made some lighthearted comment to my wife about "the twins." A few years later when I saw CW on the streets in Los Angeles, he smiled and playfully asked, "How are the twins?"

Parolee Visits

Soon after beginning my research, some of the prisoners I had come to know began being paroled. Several of them dropped by my home in Berkeley, where they visited me and my family. This usually was a social visit with them interacting with me and my family. Only occasionally did a visit entail serious matters. With a few parolees, the relationship grew and lasted for years as we became involved in the Chicano movement that had arisen on the streets. Something that was unspoken, but certainly understood by me, was that the parolees' visits confirmed that I was for real. This was conveyed to prisoners back inside San Quentin. It merely strengthened my rapport with Chicano convicts.

Secrets

CDC's Secrecy

As I indicated earlier, my initial goal as a work-study graduate student, in the summer of 1966, was to look into subcultural factors in the background of Chicano prisoners which made them excessively violent and excessively reluctant to participate in rehabilitation activities. Prison administrators did not know the Chicanos and their subculture well enough to be able to fill in the gaps in their understanding. It was obvious from their request for me to conduct research that they felt a need for such information. One administrator who was frustrated by staff inability to really get to know and understand Chicanos warned me, "They're a tough nut to crack."

I realized that establishing rapport with Chicano prisoners was the most important challenge I initially faced. I recognize several key factors contributed to my success: I went alone to almost everywhere in the prison—quite unlike the actions of any freeman, especially other researchers. I took no notes—to avoid intimidating prisoners in any way. I merely had conversations with prisoners—usually letting them do most of the talking. I never used questionnaires. I openly shared my personal background of being from a large family, of working my way through college, of having jobs from laborer, roofer, magazine salesman, journeyman meat cutter, taxi driver, to life insurance salesman. I never put myself above them. I never criticized them.

The way that I approached the Chicanos—unlike the methods used by earlier researchers— contributed to my success in establishing rapport and learning what I ultimately did. I still remain in debt to them for what they—often as friends—shared with me.

Soon after the beginning of my research, I gradually became aware of the *secrecy* and *absolute power* of prison administrators and CDC.

As staff became accustomed to seeing me almost anywhere in the prison, and as they assumed that since I had permission from administration be go virtually anywhere, I must not be a threat to them. They became somewhat relaxed when they saw me—just a researcher from U.C. Berkeley walking around the prison talking to people. Usually I talked one-on-one with non-administrators (lower level staff and guards). I let them do most of the talking, with me saying little. I learned a lot; they seemed less interested in me than I was in them. I came to realize that—after talking for a while— perhaps some needed to vent about things in the prison that they were prohibited from discussing in public. Thus, I was able to learn a great amount.

However, as I learned more about the power that prison administrators had over information from inside prison, one very important thing that *negatively* impressed me was the extent of that power. It was almost *absolute*!

True, prisoners are able to receive information *from outside*, but those sources are limited and the information definitely is one-way. Most prisoners are able to listen to either of the two local radio stations that are monitored by the prison staff and made available for prisoners. The monitored stations have a great deal of music and very little news. Also, prisoners who legally have money in their "inmate account" may subscribe to newspapers and magazines (subject to certain restrictions) which are delivered through the mail. In addition, through approved visitors and correspondents (old friends and family members) it may be possible to keep abreast of activities of friends and family on the streets.

For people on the streets—the general public and even state legislators—the flow of information *from inside* prison is limited in many ways. For example, even though outsiders may subscribe to the biweekly prison newspaper, the *San Quentin News*—where the reporting is done by and for the prisoners—staff restrictions limit the news to activities of formally approved prisoner organizations, recreational activities, and the like. These are activities that have a minimal impact on the lives and activities of most prisoners. In contrast, prisoner activities and interests that take place on the vast covert levels of the prisoner culture—things that probably would be newsworthy to outsiders—are omitted. The prisoner reporters are not allowed to write of violence, defiance of authority, or violation of prison rules.

San Quentin guards censor outgoing prisoner mail for statements about the reputation of the institution, mistreatment of inmates, criticism of law, rules or policy, and attitudes toward discontent or racial friction.

Staff members are ordered to not discuss institutional affairs off duty, or with outsiders. They are required to refer all inquiries from the public to the Office of the Warden. If a staff member should publicly criticize the prison or CDC, or openly approach a state legislator to discuss problems within the prison system or at a particular prison, that staff member is subject to being fired and actively blackballed from other similar employment.

Even outsiders who volunteer their time to work with prisoners in some way are beholden to the prison administrators for entry into the prison and would be denied entry if they publicly criticized the prison system.

A man who has just been paroled from prison is limited to what he may say publicly about prison by restrictions that are expressed in the Parole Agent Manual.

Approved visitors who do visit a prisoner are reluctant to use any information that is critical of the prison or CDC, which may be verbally shared with them by a prisoner. If the visitors should attempt to publicize such information, the prisoner who gave them the information could be severely punished for such action.

Prisoners are fully aware, and some staff members privately admit, that these and other restrictions make it almost impossible for most outsiders to know what is actually going on behind prison walls.

Prison administrators are not subject to the restrictions noted above. They know much of what goes on behind the prison walls.

However, they usually have been less than candid. They are so much a part of the system that some of them have gone to great lengths to hide or distort the reality inside prison from the public. They have perpetuated an *ideal* view of the prison system which is remote from the *real* prisoner culture that the prisoners know and experience behind the walls.

The actions of administrators generally assure that the prison remains a closed system—one that keeps both the prisoners and the truth tightly locked behind the walls. For example, most members of the news media are fully aware that a news story about prison almost always comes directly from a prison administrator—that it is never given to them *inside* the prison walls. Also, it is impossible for an outsider to casually visit a prison and talk with prisoners; he first must go through official channels. The outsider may sign up for a warden's tour, but it is impossible to even begin to see the reality of the prisoner culture on a guided tour. Regardless of what occurs inside, prison administrators have the almost absolute power to control the flow of information from within the prison. Occasionally that power has been tyrannically used to conceal or disguise the reality behind the prison walls.

For me, learning of the magnitude of incredible power to control information from within the prison by administrators was astonishing. Particularly applicable to me (an outsider or freeman) and my research was the passage from above which pointed out that *outsiders are beholden to prison administrators for entry into the prison and would be denied entry if they publicly criticized the prison system.* Early in my research, I learned many things about abuse of prisoners and some of the hidden reality behind the walls. These abuses angered my sense of fairness. And, a few of the ways that prisoners were abused and/or manipulated—outraged me!

"Silent beefs" are one of the illegal ways that staff unofficially exercise social control over prisoners. The comments a prisoner made to me illustrate both what a silent beef is and what prisoners think about them. Without committing himself as to his innocence or guilt the prisoner told me something along the lines of, "The bulls think I stabbed another inmate. They don't have any evidence for a conviction;

but since they *think* I'm guilty, I'll serve the time for the last beef too." The prisoner, quite bitterly continued, "These so-called defenders of the peace, these so-called good guys, set themselves up as God, judge, and jury. They're able to get away with convicting a man of a crime merely on a hunch, or on the word of a snitch, or on some other sort of invalid evidence. You can't fight the board on this either, because they're in cahoots with the bulls and they'll always be able to come up with something other than the real reason why they're keeping you in—why they think you aren't rehabilitated yet. You can't protest, because it's just your word against theirs; and they always win."

Another example of silent beefs occurred one day as I was having lunch outside the prison walls but still inside the prison grounds at the staff snack bar—small, attractive, with large windows affording a view of part of the San Francisco Bay. I was sitting at a table with Sergeant B and a guard. The sergeant was bragging to me about his power over prisoners. He noted how a few years earlier a particular prisoner murdered another inside the prison. Sergeant B related that there wasn't enough evidence to take the prisoner to court to convict him, but he (Sergeant B) *knew* the prisoner was guilty.

"How?" I asked.

"From my sources," he responded.

The guard jokingly interjected, "From his snitches."

Ignoring the guard's comment, Sergeant B went on to proudly explain how he had taken the average time normally served by prisoners for *this* prisoner's original sentence and added the average time for murder. Sergeant B then said, "I'm making sure the prisoner serves the total average times of both crimes combined."

I shook my head and looked puzzled.

Sergeant B explained that he personally would continue going to the board every year before the prisoner's board hearing, to make sure the prisoner served the total average time for *both* crimes. The guard smiled and nodded his approval.

Angered and frustrated, but not showing it, I bit my tongue and said nothing. To do so might have raised red warning flags for Sergeant B and possibly could have resulted in the extremely premature termination of my research.

My Anger And Frustration

As I continued to learn more and more about the secrecy and absolute power of guards, non-custody staff members, prison administrators, the Adult Authority and CDC, I kept reminding myself that much of the power to contain and control incarcerated convicted felons inside prison was legitimately necessary. However, I could not understand why abusive, or secret, or often illegal acts were frequently used against prisoners. My personal deep-seated sense of fairness was violated by some of what I was discovering. Seeing the unreasonable abuse of one human being by another heightened my outrage. The more I learned of these unbelievable illegal and abusive powers, the more my anger and frustration grew.

Personally, I realized that there was a tremendous amount of additional material to be learned before I could write a viable ethnography and accomplish what I intended to do. I did a lot of soul-searching. My research was to understand and describe *the Chicano prisoners' own culture inside prison.* My goal was to come to understand that culture as the Chicano prisoners themselves experience and perceive it—*without condemning.* From the beginning I realized I would have to suspend judgment of the prisoners' past crimes—recognizing that they are being punished by incarceration for those crimes.

I understood that *if* my research was abruptly and prematurely terminated by prison administrators, all that I had previously done would be for naught. Consequently, I determined what I *should* and should *not* do to avoid getting kicked out of San Quentin:

—I should, if possible, try to avoid talking with administrators and higher levels of Custody staff. My fear was that I'd become too involved in conversation and unwittingly reveal some of what I had planned. This led to my being cautious and somewhat secretive with staff and administrators. I purposely let them or encouraged them to do most of the talking. At times I felt like I was spying when interacting with them.

—I should constrain myself from publicly (outside of prison) saying or revealing things I could not reveal without getting kicked out, even though at times I strongly felt that such revelations should be made.

—I should be very low-key and cautious in my activities on the streets on behalf of prisoners and in the Chicano movement.

—I should be careful when discussing my intent to "tell it like it is." With *prisoners*, reveal the depths of my intent only with trusted convicts and Mexican Mafia members. With *staff*, be guarded, vague and not open like I was with certain prisoners. Let the staff do most of the talking; ask them questions if needed to keep conversations going.

At times my self-constraint would be pushed to the extreme. However, again and again, with great reluctance to **NOT** say or do what I *thought* should be said or done—and at times with some very good luck thrown in—I carefully followed my own advice which succeeded until the day before Convict Unity Holiday, February 14, 1968.

Mexican Mafia Revealed

At the beginning of my research, the relationship between prisoners and me might have been characterized as one of researcher-research*ee*. They, the researchees, were the teachers; and I, the researcher, was the student who was trying to learn their subculture—what I usually call the prisoner culture. But, with time and hours of discussion with many Chicano convicts, the relationship between them and me gradually changed to also include the element of friendship. With some, our relationship developed into one of very close personal friendship—often lasting into the years when they were paroled or discharged and on the streets.

Let me share some things about one particular Chicano convict. When I first met ML, he had spent nearly half of his 38 years of life behind prison walls. He had served, and was serving, time for the crimes he had committed. Because of his intense Chicano subcultural pride, he refused to fear or kowtow to guards, administrators, parole board members and anyone who worked for CDC who tried to control him. Consequently, he had suffered their wrath and served much more time for individual convictions than most prisoners normally do. ML was exceptionally intelligent and observant. Few, if any, convicts knew the prisoner culture better than he did. So, he was able to manipulate and use the prisoners' culture to his own advantage—in ways few other prisoners could.

In San Quentin one day, when talking with ML, my extremely close Chicano-convict-friend, he asked me to confirm what I had much earlier told him—that I was going to write a book and tell it like it is. I reassured him, that still was what I intended to do. Then, quite seriously, he asked if I knew about the Mexican Mafia. I responded that I had *heard* of it, but that was about all, admitting that I really didn't know much about it.

Then he explained that there are a lot of things—"loose ends below the surface here in prison that are *secret*, but you should know about them." Then he stressed that I could *never* reveal any of them. I acknowledged what he had said, but probably had a confused look on my face.

He explained that, *if* I know about those secret things maybe I can carefully weave them together some way to make sense out of them without ever revealing any specifics about them. I nodded agreement and made some comment about understanding what he meant.

Then ML smiled and further explained, "That way your book will be much better."

Soon ML and I were in a deep conversation. He revealed that he was one of the founding leaders of what originally was called *Baby Mafia*, then *Family* (or *Familia*). Then and later, in many conversations with him and a few key Mexican Mafia members, the door to their secrets was opened. (Now, *Mexican Mafia* is the commonly used term.)

Before the publication of *Chicano Prisoners* in 1974, the history, goals, ethics, and bylaws of *Family* existed only in oral form. Because of the seriousness of the group's activities and the resulting secrecy, no member had ever written down *Family's* history, goals, ethics, and bylaws. *Family* members knew these well, generally agreed on the important points and were able to tell them to new members. Possessing such written material would have been extremely dangerous and potentially self-incriminating.

However, those "secret loose ends below the surface" *were shared with me.* A few years later, in 1972 and '73, the previous sharing by the members of the Mexican Mafia enabled me to *carefully* write a great deal about the Mexican Mafia's history, goals, ethics, bylaws, power and *much* more in *Chicano Prisoners.* **Other than what I revealed in Chicano Prisoners *with its publication in 1974, I have not talked or written about the changes in the Mexican Mafia that have taken place since 1972, and I will adamantly continue to do so.***

In late 1972, I had already decided that I did not want to go beyond my knowledge of the Mexican Mafia at that time. I was not surprised when ML told me I should *not* try to continue following the conflict between the warring factions of the Mexican Mafia. He warned, "There's no way you can stay completely neutral. If you try to, one side or the other will take offense at something and kill you because of what you say or write. We couldn't guarantee your safety any more." ML and I agreed that it would be best for my safety—and perhaps my life—to *not* follow the changes and conflicts between the factions of the Mexican Mafia which we both foresaw. We agreed that I already had enough to complete my book—telling it like it is in San Quentin and CDC. To detail the predictable Mexican Mafia warfare would have been too dangerous and beyond the intent of my book.

At the conclusion of *Chicano Prisoners*, I noted that in late 1972 significant changes began taking place in what was called "Family" at that time. The unity of *all* members of Family, no longer existed. For some members, the loyalty to the larger (roughly 300-member) Family had come to be too much in conflict with the allegiance they felt toward their own sub-Family (usually about 25 members) or toward a kinship-related Family member (such as a cousin). This resulted in a major split in Family in 1973. The complex, opposing loyalties led to an extremely brutal power struggle that continued between *la EME* and *Nuestra Familia*, major factions of Family. Much bloodshed and many deaths occurred both in prison and on the streets. Unfortunately, it appeared that this warfare would continue below the surface and generally beyond the control of authorities for a long time into the future, with neither side being able to eliminate the other, because new members were being brought into both factions faster than they were being killed.

The bloody details of that brutal power struggle have continued for over thirty years. Those details are purposely beyond my knowledge. And, they are the reason I adamantly refuse to talk or write about the changes in the Mexican Mafia since 1973.

In 1973, ML and a few other members of the Mexican Mafia read the manuscript of *Chicano Prisoners*. They were pleased with my treatment of their group—as well as the way that I was able to tell it like it is.

When ML and I first discussed the Mexican Mafia, I shared how I had (very early in my research) realized that to broach the subject of the Mexican Mafia could have been devastating to my research. He agreed that, had I early on asked a member about the Mexican Mafia, I probably never would have been able to talk with him again. **And** he probably would have spread the word to other prisoners about this guy who was spying on Chicanos. He also agreed that had I asked some prisoner who was *not* a member of the Mexican Mafia about the group, that prisoner probably would never have talked with me again—fearful of being seen talking to some guy who was going around asking prisoners about the Mexican Mafia.

Piggybacking the above comments, ML noted that I had been lucky when I started my research, dealing almost entirely with Chicanos. He said that had I started my research by talking with Black prisoners, it would have failed. I agreed, guessing what he was about to say. However, he went on to explain anyway, noting that the Blacks generally have a reputation for snitching, so I would never have been able to establish rapport with Chicanos, who generally will not snitch. I would have been guilty by association.

RIOTOUS YEAR

RACE RIOTS, 1967

When newly-elected Governor Reagan was inaugurated in January, 1967, his first priority was to reduce the sizeable deficit that he inherited from former Governor Pat Brown. Reagan ordered a hiring freeze, *a ten percent budget cut from all state agencies* and other expenditure reductions. Administrators at San Quentin panicked—how could they cut their part of CDC's budget by ten percent? Immediately a few rumors floated, but nothing official was ever announced.

How did administrators and staff avoid those budget cuts? *They illegally, yet deliberately manipulated most of the prisoners for ulterior motives!*

The massive racial confrontation that took place at San Quentin on Wednesday, January 18, 1967 is—quite sadly—a striking example of the way that administrators and staff are able to manipulate prisoners. There were many conflicting versions of the circumstances surrounding the *so-called race riots.* Many prisoners and staff members never did believe the *official version* that prison administrators presented to the public.

My version is based on a wide variety of contacts—the most important sources were my *many* discussions with prisoners and staff members—staff members who were willing to "privately" discuss the riotous events and surrounding circumstances with me. I believe that most prisoners, as well as the majority of staff members who were at San Quentin at that time would generally agree with my version.

A minor incident on the preceding Thursday between a Black kitchen worker and a guard was construed by the Black prisoners who worked in the kitchen as an act of racial prejudice. Intense resentment of Blacks led the staff to "fire" 12 of the prisoners from their kitchen jobs on Friday. The next day, 31 additional kitchen workers went on a sympathy strike.

Black prisoners called for a strike of all Black workers on Monday. But, in order to break the strike attempt, the staff ignored the routine precautions against letting men go to jobs in the industrial area when the fog precludes surveillance of the men as they go to work; three Blacks were beaten, one Anglo was stabbed, and one Anglo was killed! Tuesday, either on principle or out of fear of retaliation, the majority of the 1,200 black prisoners refused to go to work.

By Wednesday morning, the strike had lost its momentum, was virtually over, and would have fizzled to nothing within a day or two. However, the staff "mishandled" the nearly 3,000 prisoners who gathered as usual in the upper yard after lunch to await work call. Gradually, opposing racial groups were formed. Next, a small number of rabble-rousers shouted curses from one group to another. Some of the prisoners began arming themselves with boards, pipes, and the like that they were tearing from benches, picnic tables, the small guard shack, and anything else that could be ripped apart. The guards locked all exits from the yard, trapping the majority of prisoners who were there for legitimate reasons, who merely thought of themselves as spectators to the antics of a few prisoners. Then, as the guards later claimed, they found it necessary to lay down a "wall of rifle fire" to keep the opposing groups from tearing each other apart. And by 4 P.M., the press was told that "the danger is over for today."

However this was not so for the almost one thousand Anglos and Chicanos who had been herded from the upper yard to the football field in the lower yard. After dark on that winter evening, many of the prisoners, who had been in shirt sleeves when things began at noon in the upper yard, ran to the bleachers to tear off wood to make bonfires in an attempt to keep warm.

With rifles and tear gas, the guards tried to stop this. Days later, outsiders were led to assume that the eight prisoners who were wounded by bullets or ricochet slugs came too close to the "wall of fire" in the upper yard. However, the prisoners contend that most were wounded by the guards in the lower yard.

Late that night, in groups of nine, prisoners were singled out and ordered to march away from the other prisoners. Then they were made to strip—as a precautionary measure to prevent weapons from being taken back into the blocks—and led by nine escort guards back to their cells. This was a time-consuming process. A convict who thought he was "almost frozen" when he was led from the lower yard at 3:05 A.M. claimed that the last two prisoners were stripped and led from the lower yard at 4:05 A.M.

Most prisoners bitterly complained—and many staff members generally agreed—that the abuse of prisoners during the following weeks was unnecessary. There was much more resentment toward the guards for their acts on the day of the so-called race riots than there was racial tension. Many staff members claimed that things would have rapidly cooled to normal if the prisoners had just been kept locked in their cells for a few days—often a routine measure after a prisoner strike, protest, or disturbance. However, the guards went far beyond a mere lockup; they continued their reign of abuse. Except for their sheer number, the claims of needless brutality of some guards in the following days and weeks would seem unbelievable.

The prison was closed to all but staff members for nearly six weeks. When I finally was allowed to enter San Quentin again, the major subject of discussion with prisoners and staff members frequently was the so-called race riots and the associated events. In addition to relating specific details, almost every conversation, at one time or another, turned to the many unanswered questions that arose from the events on and around January 18th. Even staff members were unable to make sense out of the actions of some guards.

For example, many staff members—including several guards who stressed the "private" nature of their discussion with me—and prisoners had some strong contentions about the lengthy buildup of opposing racial groups and hostility that preceded the "wall of fire" that the guards finally laid down to keep the opposing groups separated. It was commonly recognized that at almost any time during that long buildup, the prisoners could have been stopped in a variety of ways. For example, a guard lieutenant noted that one way to clear the yard of prisoners almost immediately is to call for a "mandatory lockup." Continuing, he stressed, "The situation in the upper yard could have been controlled earlier." The lieutenant said that officials never did adequately explain why the situation was allowed to foment to the point of violence. He indicated that there was no official censure of the associate warden, custody, or the captain (of the guards) for their handling of the situation, but that there was a "lot of unofficial criticism and gossip" among the guards. Furthermore, there was considerable awareness among the guards that the prisoners felt they had been manipulated, and some of the guards were inclined to agree with the prisoners.

Another peculiar thing reportedly occurred during the riots. Two particular prisoners played principal roles as instigators. During the buildup of opposing groups at the beginning of the riots, these two were most active. They were right out in front of the Anglo and Chicano group, cursing and threatening the Blacks while a guard was taking movies from the gun rail above the prisoners. Even if there had been no movies, prisoners are quite certain that the captain would never forget being cursed and told by the two inmates that they were in charge and, in no uncertain terms, how he should sexually abuse himself.

Later, B Section was filled with hundreds of prisoners being punished for their activities during the riots, but the two leaders were never disciplined. Instead, they were rewarded for their efforts. Prisoners claimed that one leader was discharged from Folsom Prison less that three months after the riots and that the other was paroled from San Quentin about two months after the incident. After more than a year of effort, I was finally able to confirm that one of these prisoners was paroled from San Quentin on March 21, 1967; however, there was no further record of the other prisoner who was supposedly transferred to Folsom Prison on February 3, 1967.

In addition to the other reasons to disbelieve the official account of the so-called race riots, there appeared to be two major ulterior motives that may have led the higher levels of custody staff to precipitate the prisoners into the crisis. First, a fundamental reorganization of the institutional structure (called "unitization") was being prepared for at San Quentin, which was intended to counter the sheer size of the prison and allow each cell block to function as a separate unit in many ways. *It would have effectively shifted some power and authority to the treatment staff, with a de-emphasis of custody.* The reorganization being brought about by "unitization" caused considerable anxiety and tension among many higher level custody staff members who felt that a major readjustment or shift in power was taking place in the custody-treatment relationship—a relationship that had always been *at least* tacitly antagonistic in nature. Custody faced a serious problem. How could it counter the changes that would be brought about by "unitization?" How could it regain the power that it was losing to treatment staff?

There was an additional factor which greatly intensified staff anxiety. As noted above, the newly elected Governor Ronald Reagan announced that all departments of the state government would be required to cut their budgets by 10 percent. A lieutenant later confided that the resulting fears of potential cuts in staff and programs, coupled with custody's fear of losing its position of power to treatment staff, caused a state of near panic among some of the staff on the powerful high levels of custody.

If we assume that these were the ulterior motives and that some among the high levels of custody staff were responsible for purposely allowing a minor incident to swell into a major "racial confrontation," we are, and probably always will be, without direct evidence to support the view—because those who actually were involved in this purposeful manipulation of the prisoners have too much to lose to ever admit to such dealings. In lieu of documentation, let us consider the net results of the race riots, because they were repeatedly cited by prisoners and staff members as additional indirect evidence for their belief that some staff members acted for ulterior motives.

Staff members were reluctant to discuss officially the final outcome of the race riots. However, many staff members were willing to convey "privately" what they had "picked up" from other staff members. Concerning the budget, cuts were made in the treatment programs. A custody lieutenant indicated that the strike, the rioting, the prolonged unrest after the confrontation, and the staff movies of some of those activities ultimately enabled custody to avoid cutting its budget. Instead of decreasing the number of guards, custody was able to hire additional guards and spend a large amount—reported by several sources to be about a quarter of a million dollars—for overtime pay for the guards. This supposedly was necessary to properly control the prisoners as things gradually calmed down after the riots. Some claimed that custody's budget actually was increased. Regardless of whether or not this was true, there was no question among staff members that, budget-wise, custody definitely had prevailed over treatment.

The apparent—though dubious—need to impose extraordinary control over the prisoners during and after the so-called race riots allowed custody to clearly reestablish its position of power over treatment. At the time of the riots, the situation appeared to be so critical that treatment staff were required to temporarily fill custody roles. The meager effectiveness that counselors and other treatment staff had before the riots was *greatly* diminished in the eyes of most prisoners when many members of the treatment staff took up rifles, billy clubs, and other weapons to help put down the prisoners. As a prisoner said, "We thought so before, but now there's no question about what side the counselors are on. They're just bulls too." From many similar comments, it was obvious that the prisoners had been significantly impressed. However, it was a negative impression that merely confirmed what many of them had earlier suspected.

Some members of the treatment staff later expressed their regrets about the riots. They had been extremely reluctant to do what they were ordered to do; yet, technically, maintaining custody is part of their job, *when and if necessary*. Had a treatment staff member refused to join the guards, he probably would have been fired. Subsequently, there was no doubt that custody was in control of the prison and that treatment was subordinate to custody. Also, in the area of staff power, there was no question that custody had definitely prevailed over treatment.

I openly admit that much of the evidence presented above is indirect. However, if the conclusions that so many staff members and prisoners drew from the evidence are correct, then it is obvious that a relatively small group of *custody* staff members were able to intentionally and successfully manipulate the prisoners (and many of their fellow staff members) for ulterior motives. Consequently, it can be seen that the staff's power to control the prisoners and maintain custody is an excessive, unrestrained power that also allows for, and generates, misuse of that power.

In contrast to custody's increased budget for the next year, treatment programs possibly could have suffered significant cuts. For nearly six weeks, education classes, and many other routine treatment activities were cancelled and the expenses for those normal activities were reduced or not used. Consequently, some of the budgeted funds were *not* used for normal programs, and the treatment budget for the next year potentially could have been reduced by that amount—*and* by the 10 percent reduction ordered by Governor Reagan.

Treatment staff feared the worst. So, behind the scenes, efforts were made to spend *all* the funds that had been budgeted for the current year (1967). It was interesting for me to observe how treatment staff scrambled to use as much of the currently-allocated budget as possible in order to minimize treatment budget cuts the next year.

For example, the top prison counselor approached me. He explained that—since he had picked up from earlier conversations that I fell into the "starving graduate student" realm—I might appreciate becoming involved in a plan to make some additional money. He did catch my attention. What he offered me was a part-time temporary position as a counselor at San Quentin until the existing budgeted treatment funds were exhausted.

Even though the money would have been welcome, the last thing I wanted to do was to receive a single cent from San Quentin! I had determined from the beginning of my research that I would *never* accept any payment of any kind from the prison or CDC. Never, in any way, did I want to be beholden to the prison. I felt that to do so would have tainted my research and probably destroyed any rapport I had developed with prisoners. I declined his offer.

Another attempt to spend unused treatment funds involved San Quentin's education department. It was proposed that a special evening class be established, with *three* instructors teaching a seminar-style class to a small number of select prisoners. If I recall correctly, the thrust of the class was purposely left rather vague—allowing for open-ended talks between the prisoners and instructors. I knew two of the chosen instructors who were already conducting research at San Quentin; their research was confined to the education building where each, at different times or on different days, would meet with a few prisoners for discussion in a classroom. Their research methods were *very* different from mine. The offer was made for me to be the third instructor. After the offer was made, I had a very private discussion with one of the researchers whom I already knew. He was quite explicit that using *three* instructors whom he knew was recognized by some in the education department as an excellent way to spend as much money as possible in a relatively short time. The earnings would have been quite welcome; however, I turned down the offer, not wanting to accept any money from the prison.

In 1967, after learning what I have related above about the so-called race riots and other very real abuses of prisoners by staff, I was angry. I was not in a position to openly reveal what I had learned—either to the public, or particularly to state legislators. I knew that if I made such revelations, administrators would have immediately terminated my research. Sad that I found myself in such a situation, but—with so much more to still be learned—I did want to continue my research.

However, after being abruptly kicked out of San Quentin on February 15, 1968, those constraints on what I could publicly reveal were eliminated.

Mitchell Execution, 1967

California had declared a moratorium on the death penalty, and Aaron Mitchell was to be the last man executed in the gas chamber at San Quentin. So, on April 8, 1967, Mitchell was executed. April 8th, being a Monday, and with most prisoner activities and jobs being closed down for the day because of the execution, I wanted to observe things on this atypical day.

The significant shutdown of scheduled prisoner activities and jobs resulted in many prisoners being free of any commitments. Things were strangely subdued, muted, as if someone had turned the volume down. Most movement seemed slow. Small groups aimlessly ambled around on the lower yard. Others sat in the bleachers, silent or softly talking. Everyone seemed moved by what was taking place that day. The death penalty was the predominant topic of conversations.

Large numbers of prisoners seemed at loose ends. A few said they were bored—which was obvious. One prisoner complained that there were no movies like they routinely have on the weekends.

There was one comment that strongly impressed me. I have never forgotten it. Three times during the day—at different places, with different prisoners—when talking about the death penalty I was bitterly told, ***"There are no rich men on death row!"***

(As an aside, the death penalty in California was reinstated in 1978).

Mess Hall Lunch

One day I was in the industries area talking with MC, an older, very mellow convict who had become a good friend of mine. He already had served considerable time in prison and was well respected by other prisoners. As it neared lunch time, he said, "Why don't you come to lunch with me?" As a friend, he wanted lunch in the mess hall to be *his* treat. He felt that my being seen going to lunch with him would enhance my rapport with prisoners—even many who had never met or talked with me. I told him I'd be delighted.

However, we both realized that if I did so, unannounced, the guards would be taken off guard and might do something unpredictable—probably quite negative. Consequently, we agreed that I'd better run it by upper level custody first, essentially to get their permission.

In the custody office, I talked with a Sergeant who was taken off guard by my request. He pointed out that only ministers and the like did that—on Christmas and Easter. Then he started talking about how I would pay for my lunch. I immediately said I'd gladly pay. He was in the midst of trying to figure out how I could pay or be billed for my lunch when the custody Captain walked in and heard the conversation. The Captain immediately picked up on what the conversation was about and disgustedly interrupted the Sergeant—noting that trying some absurd or complex way to have me pay for lunch a few times was insane. The Captain went on to note that "all the paperwork and time involved would cost a hell of a lot more than any crummy meal."

The Sergeant said he'd get word to the guards that normally worked in the mess hall—so they'd not panic if I came in for lunch a few times.

A few days later, I joined MC to be his guest for lunch. We joined the throng of prisoners leaving from the industries area, heading along the east side of the lower yard toward the south mess hall. The throng backed up and almost stopped when it reached the very narrow, steep, one lane alleyway that delivery trucks climbed to deliver food and supplies to the mess halls. There was a sea of blue as the mass of prisoners slowly moved forward. I had never gone this way before, so MC noted that—even though there was a guard high above on a gun rail who could observe the prisoners—they were so packed so tightly that it was a dangerous place. Prisoners had often been shanked (stabbed) without the guard seeing. He noted that one time a prisoner who had been shanked was finally seen by the guard, lying dead in a pool of blood after the throng of prisoners had walked over and around his body.

MC and I joined the line going into the south mess hall. As we actually entered along the east wall, I heard several catcalls and shouts, above the low roar of conversations; but those soon stopped. On the cafeteria line, the prisoners serving the food to me were quite surprised—it wasn't Easter, and I wasn't a minister. I assumed the guards had received the word, because they seemed to tolerate my presence.

After the "crummy" lunch, MC and I talked as we left the mess hall and walked to the upper yard. He said he was surprised that there were only a few catcalls and shouts when I entered the mess hall. He had expected that their might have been a lot of catcalls and noise. Then he added that he hadn't realized how much my reputation must have spread among convicts.

A few weeks later I again joined MC for lunch. This time, when we entered the mess hall, not a single catcall or shout was heard. I made some comment about the relative silence above the normal low roar of conversations. MC merely responded, "We passed the word around."

Conflict With Extreme Conservatism In Anthropology

In the spring of 1967, when talking with Professor George Foster—my doctoral committee chairman at UC Berkeley—regarding what I should do in the future about revealing what I was learning about Chicano prisoners and the depths of the prisoners' own largely illegal and rule-breaking subculture at San Quentin, I was shocked and will never forget when he told me to ***"Accentuate the positive and eliminate the negative!"*** I could not believe what he had said! Not wanting to misinterpret the meaning of what he had said, I pressed him for clarification. Essentially he wanted me to avoid ever revealing things that would embarrass San Quentin and CDC administrators. This was appalling to me. His opinion went against some deeply-felt beliefs that I had about the nature of anthropological research. I found it virtually impossible to believe what he had told me. I seriously wondered how I could continue in my doctoral studies with him as my committee chairman.

Within the next few days I had personal conversations with three other professors in the department—I had taken courses from them and/or worked with and consulted with them regarding my research. I had developed excellent rapport with each of them. Professors Gerald Berreman, Octavio Romano and James Anderson each understood my dilemma.

They *privately* revealed several things to me. Foster was among the oldest and certainly the most conservative anthropologist in the department. Foster was extremely influential and powerful in the department—more so than any other professor. I would fail to earn my doctorate if I did not go along with his wishes—he would thwart my efforts. My *Geographic* area of specialty was Mexico, including Meso-America. My two *Subject* areas of specialty were Peasantry as a societal type, and Applied Anthropology. These were Foster's specialties too. Consequently, the three professors agreed that I would not be able to avoid Foster as I continued my doctoral studies in the department, and none of them had the political clout in the department to fight against Foster and win on my behalf.

Since it was sadly unrealistic for me to continue in the doctoral program at Berkeley, they suggested I approach some of the professors in the Anthropology Department at U.C. Davis. That department was not constrained by the extreme conservatism of any individual such as Foster, and transferring into the Davis doctoral program should be quite easy.

I talked with Professors David Olmsted, Daniel Crowley, David Smith and Richard Curley who were excited about my truly unique research. Being younger and more liberal, they strongly disagreed with Foster's admonition to me that I "accentuate the positive and eliminate the negative." They facilitated my transfer to U.C. Davis during the summer of 1967. They agreed that I should wait until I would be ready to reveal *all* of the prisoners' own subculture—including elements of CDC's secrecy and abuse of prisoners which were a very real part of the prisoners' experience in their subculture. They recognized that when I wrote my dissertation and/or ethnography, that would be the appropriate time to "tell it like it is." Professor Dave Olmsted became chairman of my doctoral committee.

(Much later, Dave became a member of the four- or five-person Ethics Committee of the American Anthropological Association which was formed to delve into the abuse of anthropologists and their research by the CIA during the Vietnam War. This will be further treated in my Conclusion at the end of this memoir.)

Machismo And Murder

I had several conversations with a Chicano convict (QK) who had come from the El Paso area. He was concerned about a fellow Chicano convict-friend (JT) who also was from the same area. JT had been convicted of killing his freeman work supervisor in the prison clothing factory in 1965. The California State Supreme Court was to review JT's case to see if his conviction for murder should stand. QK and many other Chicano prisoners wanted to generate support on the streets to have the conviction overturned. *And,* if not enough was being accomplished on the streets, the Chicanos planned to create a demonstration inside to support JT's case. *So,* QK approached me to see what I could do to help.

As in other situations—when I did things on the streets on behalf of prisoners inside—I had to weigh the risk of administrators finding out about my *outside* of prison efforts which often revealed things about *inside* prison events. If these efforts were discovered and judged as negative *by administrators,* they could have immediately barred me from entering San Quentin again. Consequently, what I did was purposely discreet and at times in secret.

In order for you, the reader, to fully understand some of the following, it is best that you know about *gunsels,* so let me describe them. Gunsels (also called low riders) are the younger, immature hoodlum element among the prisoners. Gunsels are the rip-off artists who take unfair advantage of other prisoners. They will burn or cheat others whenever possible. Even when caught doing illegal things by bulls, the negative consequences leave them shameless. In fact, their punishment is something to brag about among fellow gunsels. They are highly individualistic, with no real regard for any kind of larger group. However, they do take pride in their dealings with convicts. They are *not* snitches; so they can be trusted by convicts—even though they really cannot be controlled.

(*Please note*: as I indicated earlier when I was treating how I started my research, since 1959 when I filed for divorce, I have *not* had access to my field notes, so a few particulars of the following are somewhat vague in my memory. However, my interaction with gunsels in the upper yard and my later treatment by the guard are seared into my memory—events that I will never forget.)

First, let me focus briefly on *machismo*—as manifest on the streets and in prison—because it pertains directly to my actions on behalf of JT in 1967.

For Chicano prisoners, the dominant characteristic trait to which their distinctive behavior is either directly or indirectly related is *machismo.* It is the fundamental concept on which basic ideas concerning acceptable masculine behavior rest. *The complex behavioral manifestations of machismo may involve qualities of masculinity, virility, honor, bravery, pride and dignity.*

Chicano prisoners often noted two related problems that many Chicanos face—*the use of drugs and the lack of qualifications to earn a decent living.* These issues form what can be called a *poverty-drug syndrome.* This syndrome is a significant manifestation of how the Chicano subculture and the larger United States culture are in conflict.

Pre-adult use of drugs such as marijuana is usually done to gain peer group acceptance—such as from local *barrio* gangs—and is culturally accepted by the many young Chicanos. Use of heavy drugs such as heroin is not generally approved by the larger Chicano community. However, use of heavy drugs is considered as acceptable behavior by some in the Chicano subculture. Peer group use of drugs is perceived as *macho* activity by those involved in such use. Unfortunately, numerous young Chicanos go to prison for their drug use. In prison, drug use may continue and possibly increase to heavy drugs if not already so.

The subcultural experiences of many Chicanos leave them in a disadvantaged condition. Many are unqualified to hold a decent job. Legitimate opportunities for decent-paying jobs are dismal for poorly-educated men with less than acceptable job training. Many find themselves in a trap of poverty. Illegal acts—including drug use as an escape—are frequently brought about by circumstances. However—to the Chicanos driven to illegal acts—those acts may be regarded as self preservation which is basic to their survival.

Several times, when engaged in deep, private conversation with a Chicano. I would be privy to soul-baring stories about "illegal" acts. The loss of *machismo* involved in those acts was so embarrassing and so emotional, that some men were ashamed to mention similar experiences to anyone—some not even to themselves. Personally, I felt extremely fortunate that my rapport was deep enough with many prisoners that they felt sufficiently comfortable to share their deep personal experiences with me.

One young Chicano related that when he was on parole, the best job that he could get when being honest to his employer about being on parole paid only $25.00 a week. (Personally I immediately wondered how he could eat and have a place to sleep on such incredibly meager pay.) He instantly went on to explain why his parole had been violated, sending him back into prison by adding, "I finally had to write some bad checks, because I just couldn't make it when our third child was born." Being *macho*, he could not let his wife and children go hungry or not have a roof over their heads. But his *machismo* also led back to prison.

Another Chicano, HD, from the Oxnard area explained how—when he became a member of a local gang—he did the expected, *macho* thing and used marijuana. Later his drug use led to heroin, arrest and prison. A few years later, when he was paroled, he was determined to *not* get involved in drug use again. HD sadly explained how the only people he knew were from his old neighborhood. At first he avoided them, not wanting to get involved in drug use again. After weeks of intense loneliness, he finally contacted some of his old friends. At first he refused their urging to use heroin with them, but he felt like an outsider. In time, in response to his friends' urging, he decided to just chip—use only a bit on an occasional basis—without getting hooked. That did not last for long, and soon he was again addicted. Arrest and prison followed. HD sadly admitted that he still had not figured out what to do when he gets paroled again. He feared his loneliness would again defeat his good intentions.

A Chicano from the Modesto area—legally here in the states, but with no job skills beyond being a farm laborer—related in heavily-accented English how he was unable to get any job during one winter. He was desperate. His wife offered to try to get a job as a waitress or something. This was a blow to his *machismo*, because he should be able to support his wife. In desperation his wife looked for work, but was unable to find a job. Unknown to him at the time, she was propositioned, brought home money and lied to him. This became a regular source of income for them. Soon however, she told him the truth. Emasculated, no longer *macho*, he turned to alcohol and then drugs as an escape. Then he was arrested, served time in prison and learned illegal ways to make money. When finally paroled, he tried, but was unable to legally make it in any way. So he turned to illegal activities and was able to remain *macho* and escape both drug use and poverty. His wife no longer had to turn tricks. Then, arrest and

San Quentin. Unfortunately, when I knew him, his wife had stopped visiting him. I saw him as a depressed, defeated individual regarding his life on the streets—but one who had learned how to survive quite well in the prisoner culture.

Most Chicanos in street gangs on the streets or in prison speak both English and Spanish, and they are able to informally communicate day-to-day things satisfactorily using colloquial speech. However, formal English or Spanish may prove difficult for them to use—either in speech or writing. More than once, when discussing this with a Chicano, I commented, "Some Chicanos have the advantage/ disadvantage of being bilingual." Usually I went on to explain that it is a distinct advantage to be able to understand and speak two languages, *but it is a disadvantage to not be able to speak or write or understand either language well.* This was recognized by many Chicano prisoners, and was one of the principal reasons for the formation of EMPLEO by Chicano prisoners—both in prison and later on the streets. (I will treat EMPLEO in detail later.)

For Chicanos who are unable to use English effectively beyond colloquial speech, and particularly for those who are not too adept at using even colloquial English, discussing or arguing important things with someone who is quite competent in English can be daunting. Actually it is a blow to a Chicano's pride, his *machismo*, to be put down in a discussion or lose an argument. His pride and dignity are challenged. This inability to effectively argue a point may lead to a pattern of silence in order avoid losing. Or, losing an argument and being personally humiliated may lead a defeated Chicano to resort to violence.

Another, very important cause of violence by Chicano prisoners is when someone unjustly, yet earnestly, insults a group's image or an individual's *machismo*.

Now, turning to JT, who was convicted of killing his freeman work supervisor in the prison clothing factory in 1965. The Chicano prisoners did not necessarily condone JT's act, but they poignantly understood the reasons behind his actions. Discussion with several Chicanos who personally knew him revealed the following important facts. JT had lived the majority of his life somewhat separated from the

Anglo culture. Primarily, he spoke Spanish, and had never learned to express himself or communicate well in English. His education ended before junior high school. He was extremely quiet and poker-faced.

The day of the killing, this man's supervisor was going to write JT up on a sex beef. JT denied involvement in a sex offense; but he failed in arguing his case with his supervisor who insisted that it was his duty to report the offense. Soon, having been unjustly accused of a sex beef—a distinct challenge to his *machismo*—and having failed to win his argument, JT's long-smoldering frustration, resentment, and hostility exploded in the killing of his supervisor—the immediate symbol of authority.

Before being taken to the captains office, where a confession was obtained, JT was taken to the Adjustment Center for thirty minutes where he was beaten by about six guards. The Chicanos who knew him well claim that each time the guards hit him, he cursed them, but did not ask for mercy. JT said he would rather have died first.

From this example, it can be seen that JT's seething hostility and inability to express himself, coupled with an unjustified threat to his *machismo*, led him to erupt in a *macho* act and to maintain his *machismo* even when being beaten by guards.

Turning back to QK's request to see what I could do to help on JT's behalf, let me continue.

In Berkeley, I made phone calls, met and talked with a few people, and discovered what I could about efforts on the streets on JT's behalf. In San Quentin, I shared what I had discovered with QK, who was satisfied with what was being done.

Closer to the actual scheduled day for the review of JT's case by the California State Supreme Court, I was approached by a young Chicano prisoner who knew me. He impatiently wanted to know what was actually happening at that time. He pressed me to do a few things that very night so I could update him the following day. I personally felt the rush to get the information for him was imposing an unreasonable deadline for me—I might not be able to contact certain individuals that evening. However, I told the young Chicano I'd try. We agreed that I'd walk into the upper yard near the end of lunch break and—since I would be in a suit and quite obvious compared to the throng of prisoners there—he'd keep an eye out for me so we could talk.

The "young Chicano" who had pressured me the day before actually was a gunsel. He picked me out of the crowd of prisoners. We walked to the northwest part of the upper yard to talk. Almost immediately a couple other Chicano gunsels joined us for a hushed, but very intense conversation. Soon, other very serious Chicano gunsels gathered— about a dozen circled closely around me—to listen. I had seen some of them, but never had talked with almost all of them—for them to have done so would not have been acceptable among other gunsels. I was surprised to be with such an unusual gathering of gunsels. Except for a few quick questions, I did most of the talking, explaining what had been done on the streets on JT's behalf. After about ten minutes of obviously intense but hushed conversation, apparently satisfied with what I had related, the gunsels quickly moved away and seemed to vanish into the throng of prisoners.

Standing alone, I quickly left the upper yard and slipped into the nearby education building to visit with CG, a prisoner-friend of mine who worked in the education book room. I rapidly went down the narrow stairs a couple flights to the entrance to the isolated book room. I knocked on the door which was closed and locked from inside for CG's safety. CG opened the door which he re-locked. Soon we were sitting on stools engaged in conversation, with me at the rear of the narrow room and CG near the door.

After twenty minutes or more, there was a very loud pounding on the door. When CG anxiously unlocked and opened the door, he was face-to-face with one of the guards from the upper yard. CG moved back many steps from the furious guard who stood in the doorway. The guard pointed and yelled, "Get out here! I wanna talk to you!"

CG said "Okay," as he started toward the door.

However, the guard yelled "No!" He pointed around CG toward me and angrily demanded, "You! It's you I wanna talk to. You come here!"

I was alarmed, not knowing if he was enraged by my earlier meeting with gunsels on the upper yard or what. Perhaps someone overheard what I was relating to the gunsels and immediately snitched to the guard. Within moments I was standing near him. CG had moved back and was watching the guard interrogate me, treating me as he might deal with a prisoner.

The guard almost accusingly said that he had "one hell of a time" tracking me down from when I left the upper yard—as if I was trying to hide from him. I merely explained that I had quickly come here to talk with CG.

The guard then demanded to know who I was and what I was doing. I hesitated to respond. This was something I did *not* want to do. My mind raced. I didn't want to inadvertently reveal too much to this angry guard and bring a premature end to my research. My rapport with prisoners was sound. However, a critical part of my rapport hinged on what I had (somewhat in confidence) shared with GC and many other prisoners—that I was going to write a book and *tell it like it is.* The guard angrily repeated his demand.

Finally, I rather clumsily said something about why I originally had been asked by administrators to come in and study Chicano prisoners, and how I had stayed to learn more about Chicanos and write a book about the prison culture. I was careful to *not* use the phrase "tell it like it is." Apparently my explanation satisfied the still-angry guard and he left.

I felt that the guard may have thought about previous descriptions of prison cultures by researchers who focused on many things that were *not* what I intended to treat in my book. Apparently he judged that my intent was not a threat. Little did he know that I was going to describe the prisoners' own largely illegal and rule-breaking culture, something unique in prison descriptions.

Also, I was extremely relieved that he apparently, in his anger, forgot to ask me what I was telling the gathering of gunsels in the upper yard. For me, answering that in some passable manner would have been quite a challenge.

I stayed. CG and I discussed the guard's visit and what had led up to the guard initially treating me as he might a prisoner. My rapport had not been damaged in any way. However, for a few minutes, the incident had been quite emotional for me.

Later, JT's Supreme Court review was *not* favorable. Unfortunately, his conviction still stood.

HOME BREW

Late one morning I went to the alley and visited SB, a convict-friend who worked in the kiln as the clerk. Usually he and I, being the only ones there, would have long conversations. The kiln was a huge, warm, dingy storage area where lumber for inside construction was stored away from the elements and kept dry. SB's job was rather boring, with lumber being brought in or taken out infrequently. This gave us privacy for our relaxed conversations in his tiny office.

Before lunch, one-by-one, several Chicano prisoners quietly slipped in and gathered into a couple of small groups that stood near some of the stacks of lumber, softly talking and frequently looking toward the office where SB and I continued our conversation. I knew a few of the new arrivals, but some I had not met. As SB and I continued talking, I became curious, but not worried. I wondered what was going on—this was not normal. Gradually the new arrivals appeared to be restless—their glances toward me increased.

Finally SB stood up and excused himself for a moment. When he returned he handed me a large plastic, electrical tape-insulated "cup" (used throughout the prison for both cold and hot drinks). As I looked to see what was inside, he said "Try it."

I did. It was tomato-based home brew. I licked my lips, smiled and said, "It's good."

Suddenly there was a flurry of activity as the new arrivals rushed to a five gallon container that had been hidden and rapidly dipped their cups in to quickly drink and then enjoy many refills of their home brew before going to lunch.

SB explained that some of the new arrivals had not been certain how I would react and were reluctant to start drinking before they had a sign. My positive reaction was the signal to them to drink and enjoy.

The kiln was an ideal place to make home brew. It was warm—to speed the brewing. It was rather dingy inside—to make it difficult for guards to see what was hidden in the depths of the stacked lumber. And guards seldom came inside. The new arrivals had trickled in on purpose so it would not draw attention to their gathering.

SB offered me a refill. I thanked him for the offer, but declined, noting that later I could go home and have a drink. This way, they would have more to drink. (Actually, I was reluctant to drink much—wanting to avoid any effects from alcohol and to remain completely aware of what I was doing.) Later, when the home brew was gone, one-by-one the now-slightly tipsy new arrivals trickled out.

When I started to leave, one particular convict, LW, said he'd leave with me. He was *very* tipsy. I did a serious double take—I felt like refusing to leave with him, but did not show my reluctance as I left with him.

LW had an interesting relationship with the Captain (of the guards). As a "runner" who delivered paperwork to and from the Captain's office, LW went virtually anywhere in the prison, and his movements never seemed to be questioned by custody. At first my suspicion of him was extreme—his being tolerated by custody *and* his being recognized as a convict by other convicts. Gradually I learned that Custody thought they were getting key information about illegal activities of prisoners from him; so it was worthwhile to give him considerable latitude. In reality though, LW was a master manipulator of information. He *would* snitch-like reveal secrets to custody. However, he was aware of so much that was illegally occurring inside that he revealed only things that very soon or simultaneously would become known to staff some *other* way. LW had perfected his timing to such a degree that custody held him in high regard as a snitch.

Back to leaving the kiln with LW. My fear was that the guard on the wall at the end of the alley would see us together. As we left the kiln and started toward the end of the alley, LW put his arm around my shoulder. LW was staggering drunk! I rather unsuccessfully tried to keep the *two* of us from weaving. I knew the guard saw us but did nothing. LW turned to go up a short hill to the Portal Plaza. As I was trying to figure out a way to leave LW's company, a convict I knew well came the other way. I told him I wanted to talk with him, so LW and I parted company, leaving him to stagger alone to the Portal Plaza where his presence would be obvious to the guards.

CHICANO SELF-HELP

BEMA CLASS

Let me point out what I personally observed, learned from prisoners, and now sincerely believe about rehabilitation activities in San Quentin. Many of those activities do *little if anything* to accomplish the broader goals of rehabilitation, failing to adequately consider the *most* important thing that all prisoners must do—*learn to survive in the prisoners' own largely illegal and rule-breaking culture twenty-four hours a day.* The next thing that seemed to often be neglected was the *real* world that prisoners would face when on the streets again.

One significant exception to the general failure of rehabilitation efforts is found in the education building. For example, if teachers can take a non-literate prisoner and teach him to read and write, that is positive. If a dropout can earn a high school diploma, that too is positive.

An example of rehabilitation failure that negatively impressed me was the carpentry class. A group of prisoners were constructing a house which was slightly larger than a child's play house—kitchen, bathroom and all. The incredibly slow pace of activity was unrealistic. When the prisoners were framing the miniature house—under the guidance of the freeman instructor—they seemed to debate exactly where each nail should be placed. After agreement, then it was decided which prisoner had the next turn to drive the nail. The driving of the nail seemed to involve a series of ten or more very light taps of a hammer to completely drive the nail. Having worked in construction years earlier, I was appalled. On a *real* job on the streets, with speed being a necessary consideration, a carpenter, almost instinctively places the nail in the proper place and then immediately drives it in with probably two heavy blows of his hammer. Routinely I would pass the tiny house, but it never seemed any closer to completion.

Attending group counseling sessions and religious activities may have positive value for some prisoners. However, many prisoners will openly admit that these activities are merely ways to please the parole board or a way to get out of their cells for a bit in the evening or on the weekends. And for some, they are reluctant to say very much or bare their souls in front of other prisoners—particularly in group counseling sessions.

While I was at San Quentin, a few prisoners even used the chapel and their *declared* religious interest as a front for illegal activity. With tremendous effort, they successfully dug a tunnel *almost* to the outside. They missed slightly, coming up short and being discovered.

The Basic Education for Mexican-Americans class (BEMA class) was started by Chicano prisoners who wanted to do something that was not being done by the staff in San Quentin. The initial efforts to establish BEMA class started about the same time that the Chicano movement on the streets began in 1966. At that time, "Mexican-American" was the *official* and *only* term used by San Quentin administrators and CDC. That never changed. Consequently, even if the founders of the BEMA class had wanted to call it Basic Education for *Chicanos* class, administrators would not have given their permission. So, to be given approval to even have the class and to hold it in an education building classroom at a given time each week, "Mexican-American" had to be used in the title.

The Chicano prisoners who started the class recognized that many Chicano prisoners have what I call the "advantage/disadvantage" of being bi-lingual. In other words, they may be able to speak Spanish and/or English well enough to get along to some degree on the streets and in prison. That is an advantage they have over many non-Chicanos who speak only English. However, not knowing either language well, they are unable to speak or write either language as proficiently as a well-educated person would. That is a disadvantage.

For those "advantaged/disadvantaged" Chicanos to use their limited command of English among non-Chicanos who are more proficient in English, it may prove to be an embarrassing disadvantage if they appear to, or feel that they do, have inferior verbal ability. To be judged inferior would be an attack on their pride and *machismo*. Consequently, they may be hesitant to try to discuss or argue about some things with someone who has a much better command of either language. Because of this, some Chicanos appear to be impassive, saying little when among non-Chicanos, particularly in most classroom settings.

I knew several of the Chicano prisoners who were involved in teaching or attending the BEMA class, which was held on Sundays in a large upstairs room in the education building. At their invitation, I attended one of their sessions. I was extremely impressed with the forty or more quite interested and involved Chicano students who were in attendance. None of the student-prisoners appeared to be ashamed of their poor language skills—to be openly involved with fellow Chicano prisoners who had similar language deficiencies was not seen as a challenge to their *machismo*. All of them recognized their need and willingly participated to increase their language skills.

A large, double-sided portable blackboard divided the room. Two dedicated, very articulate and well-educated Chicano convicts were instructing the students. On one side of the room, using one side of the blackboard, basic Spanish was being taught by one of the instructor-prisoners. On the other side, basic English was being taught by the other instructor-prisoner. I merely observed the intense interest and activity. Surprisingly the blackboard did work to effectively divide the single room. Even the shaking of the blackboard when being erased from the opposite side was ignored. I was greatly impressed with how worthwhile this was for all these men.

Within a couple of weeks, at the invitation of the instructor-prisoners, I attended another Sunday meeting of the BEMA class. This time they wanted me to give a pep talk—sharing my positive evaluation of their class with the prisoners. It was a pleasure to share my sincere enthusiasm with them.

Much later, I talked with Dr. Ralph Guzman (who at that time was Assistant Director of the Mexican-American Study Project at the University of California, Los Angeles). Finally, in January, 1968, he brought three of his Chicano graduate students with him to visit a special three-hour non-teaching Sunday meeting with the Chicanos in the BEMA class. Five hours of discussion in my home and the three-hour meeting in San Quentin left Dr. Guzman and his students astonished. Ralph admitted that he and his graduate students had no real idea of the grass roots element of the Chicano population from which most of the Chicano prisoners come. He acknowledged that even though this part of the Chicano population might show up in much of the statistical material of his project, there virtually was no contact with them by researchers in his project.

I realized that Ralph and his graduate students probably were from a small, different segment of the Chicano population in the Los Angeles area. They were likely to be from a non-barrio, better-educated part of the population—which was perceived as being *upper class* by grass-root (or weed-root) Chicanos. One of the graduate students who visited San Quentin with Ralph that January continued his education and became Director of Chicano Studies at Stanford University.

It is a tribute to the influence of that visit with prisoners in the BEMA class *and* to Ralph, that he continued to learn more about Chicano prisoners and Chicanos from the barrios. Ralph and I had a warm, fruitful relationship for many years.

Empleo

Empleo, the name of a Chicano self-help organization that Chicano prisoners formed inside San Quentin Empleo means:

In Spanish		In English
E =	**E**l =	The
M =	**M**exicano =	Mexican
P =	**P**reparado =	Prepared
L =	**L**isto =	Ready
E =	**E**ducado =	Educated
O =	**O**rganizado =	Organized

Some of the same Chicano prisoners who were involved in the BEMA class became active in the formation of Empleo. They wanted to form a Chicano self-help organization that would help Chicano prisoners—both while they were in prison and when they were again on the streets. This was to be an approved organization inside San Quentin and soon would be functioning on the streets too, so it was required to have a constitution and be approved by Warden Nelson.

The demands of writing a constitution for Empleo that would be approved by Administration, Custody and the Warden were considerable. A tremendous amount of time and effort were devoted to writing their constitution. I had several conversations with the prisoners involved, but *they* were the ones who finally produced their seven-page, detailed constitution—it was completely *their* organization. Prison staff was *not* involved—only Chicano prisoner volunteers. One of the prisoners involved in the writing of the constitution and the subsequent success of Empleo was CW, whom my wife met when we attended the dinner and talent show in the south mess hall in early September, 1966. CW was deeply committed and active in both the BEMA class and Empleo. Later he was a vigorous supporter of Empleo after he was paroled and it began functioning on the streets in the Los Angeles area.

The purpose of Empleo was multi-faceted: Get Mexican-Americans a job upon release from prison and to keep them from returning to any penal institution. Increase their job opportunities. Develop, maintain and better their communications and education. Improve their relations with administration. Help them acquire confidence, knowledge and understanding of different job problems inside and outside of prison. Further dedicate them to the purpose of becoming better citizens. At all times place their minds and bodies to this dedication of Empleo and reach their hands in friendship and in honesty to all persons, regardless of race, color or creed.

The constitution of Empleo was written to guide its members in the furtherance of their aims and desires, enabling them to find a better life—a life more suitable to their talents.

Personally I found the long-sustained, deep concern and dedication of some Chicano prisoners to helping their fellow Chicanos—both in prison and on the streets—to be quite admirable. For many years after I was kicked out of San Quentin and CW (mentioned above) was paroled in 1968, I would occasionally run into him in the Los Angeles area. He would always begin by jokingly asking, "How are the twins?" Then, in response to my questioning he would update me about his efforts to counsel gang members, to befriend hardened teenagers and to cool violent tempers. He openly admitted to those "youngsters" that he had messed up his own life. He now was doing anything he could to get those "young kids" to avoid repeating his own mistakes.

Prisoner protest

The Outlaw

The Outlaw, the prisoners' own newspaper, was a result of the extreme frustrations prisoners faced when trying to counter San Quentin's and CDC's ability to control information from inside the prison. (My earlier section on "CDC's Secrecy" is quite pertinent here.)

Illegal and truly underground, *The Outlaw* rose from the covert depths of the prisoners' own culture, beginning in June, 1967 and—having accomplished its major objective—voluntarily ending publication after 14 months in August, 1968. It reported things that were very important to the majority of prisoners, important to taxpayers and legislators, but threatening to the status quo of CDC and San Quentin. The serious articles in *The Outlaw* dealt with the *real* prisoner culture, not with the *ideal* one about which administrators spoon-fed information to the public—*including state legislators.*

Throughout CDC, prison administrators had long-been able to minimize and almost completely avoid the *real* issues behind work strikes and protests by prisoners. As I learned more about those *real* issues and the unsuccessful attempts of prisoners who attempted to publicize those issues, *I too became frustrated and angry!*

For example, early in my research ML, who had already become my extremely close Chicano-convict friend, suggested I read original memos from 1963 that were written by administrators at Folsom

Prison. The memos were hidden from public view in a San Quentin prisoner's record jacket. This prisoner had been one of the leaders of the October, 1963 work strike by prisoners at Folsom prison. The *real* strike issues involved policies and actions of the Adult Authority that prisoners felt were abusive. However, Folsom administrators had been able to avoid the major issues behind the strike. *Publicly*—as revealed in my newspaper review of the *San Francisco Chronicle* and *Sacramento Bee* for that period—prison administrators repeatedly indicated that the prisoners were striking for better food, more pay for their prison jobs, and shorter prison terms. The *real* issues were never mentioned.

Temporarily jumping ahead to 1973, in order to further illustrate the ability of prison administrators to control what information is released to the public about events inside San Quentin, let me share my disappointment. In 1973 when prisoners at San Quentin did *not* have *The Outlaw* as their spokesman, prisoners went on strike. The prisoners had a list of 17 demands. Some *still-important* demands included issues such as abolition of the Adult Authority, abolition of the indeterminate sentence system and legal representation for prisoners at parole hearings. Those issues were virtually ignored in what was spoon-fed to the media by administrators. Instead, less important, but more colorful demands—such as resignation of the warden and two associate wardens, conjugal visits and public phones inside—were stressed.

Also, administrators found that the easiest way to minimize the effect of protest against the prison or CDC was to discredit the prisoners who led protests by calling them "militants" or "revolutionaries." This tactic also was used against outsiders who openly demonstrated in support of prisoners. The outsiders also were called "militants" or "revolutionaries," thus discrediting them too.

Now, returning to 1967 and 1968, let me share some more facts about *The Outlaw*, because it was the driving force behind Convict Unity Holiday. Despite all staff attempts to suppress *The Outlaw*, ML (one of the editors) and the other prisoners who published it were determined to try to accomplish something that had never before occurred.

At first *The Outlaw* was able to print hundreds of copies of each edition, using the prison mimeograph machines. Soon the staff put all such machines under lock and key, but that did not stop the prisoners' efforts—locks and keys were no deterrent. However, the price of mimeograph stencils, paper and ink skyrocketed—again, no deterrent to the determination of the publishers and their supporters. Even when the mimeograph machines were so heavily controlled by staff that they normally were beyond the use of prisoners, and when stencils were doled out through sign up sheets, the publishers prevailed. True, by this time tall stacks of *The Outlaw* no longer "appeared" inside each cell block; however single-sheet editions were distributed to convicts. Those single sheet editions were repeatedly passed from prisoner to prisoner. Also, a copy of each edition *appeared* on the Warden Nelson's desk!

Any prisoner who was caught by the guards with a copy of *The Outlaw* in his possession was "thrown in the hole" for 29 days—no questions asked. Prisoners who were believed to be directly involved in its publication were transferred to other prisons and put in the hole there. (A convict who was *accused* by the staff of being the editor spent nearly two years in the adjustment center at Folsom because of that allegation which was not true). Even after 50 or more convicts had been transferred to other prisons, *The Outlaw* continued.

Personally, I was amused that the staff tried to defeat *The Outlaw* head-on. I had an idea that would have soon destroyed the effectiveness of *The Outlaw*. However, I *never* shared my idea with the staff. I realized that, *if the staff produced* many outrageously fictitious editions of *The Outlaw* and had their snitches distribute them to prisoners, the majority of prisoners would perhaps be amused at the ridiculous stories but would soon realize that *The Outlaw* (both legitimate and fictitious ones) was merely a joke and not to be trusted.

Although ML and the other convicts who published *The Outlaw* hoped that some editions would reach the streets and be brought to the attention of the public, they were not sure if their efforts were being noted on the streets. They realized that a way they might be able to draw more attention to their cause and exert more pressure on the prison administrators would be to successfully publicize some of the major problems facing the prisoners and try to bring even more attention to their concerns by a demonstration inside and the publicity that might ensue. So, a January 1968 issue of *The Outlaw* set forth the details about Convict Unity Holiday. I'll quote from my copy of that edition. Note, each edition had the same large, hand-lettered banner.

The OUTLAW
BY
BEEEK

SAN QUENTIN—JANUARY—1968 B.C.

ON FEBRUARY 15,1968, THOSE AREAS WHICH WILL BE EXEMPT FROM THE MOVEMENT WILL BE AS FOLLOWS: THESE AREAS ARE ESSENTIAL AND SHOULD CONTINUE TO OPERATE.

1. <u>HOSPITAL</u> 2. <u>MESS-HALL</u> 3. <u>BOILER ROOM</u> 4. <u>BLOCK WORKERS</u>

LET US TAKE THE OPPORTUNITY TO ASSURE EACH AND EVERYONE OF YOU THAT WE CAN BE SUCCESSFUL IF, AND ONLY IF, WE REMAIN UNITED. THE EFFORTS OF EACH MAN WILL BE VITAL TO THE ULTIMATE OUTCOME. ON FEBRUARY 15, 1968, THE EYES OF MANY PEOPLE WILL FOCUS UPON YOU, CONVICTS AND FREE PEOPLE ALIKE, ANXIOUSLY AWAITING TO SEE IF WE HAVE THE ABILITY AND COURAGE TO STAND UP FOR SOMETHING WORTHWHILE. LET'S NOT DISAPPOINT THEM. ABOVE ALL, LET US NOT DISAPPOINT OURSELVES. UNITY, THAT'S WHAT WE NEED.

...WE MUST NOT RESORT TO ANY TYPE OF VIOLENCE; OTHERWISE WE WILL DESTROY WHAT WE HAVE WORKED SO HARD TO GAIN. WE, OF THE OUTLAW, HAVE TAKEN MANY CHANCES IN KEEPING YOU POSTED ON THE EVILS WHICH EXIST WITHIN THE ADMINISTRATION. NOW, WE OFFER YOU A FEW OF THE THINGS WE EXPECT TO GAIN, IF WE STAND TOGETHER. REMEMBER, ON

FEBRUARY 15, 1968 ON CALL FOR LOCKUP, GO TO YOUR CELL. DO NOT BECOME INVOLVED IN ANYTHING. THIS IS IMPORTANT. THE FIRST SIGN OF A DISTURBANCE, THIS ADMINISTRATION WILL FIRE TEAR GAS AND BULLETS. SOME WILL BE INJURED, AS WE PANIC IN AN ATTEMPT TO SCATTER. WE MUST NOT PERMIT THIS. IF NO LOCKUP IS CALLED ON THIS DAY, THE SAME MOVEMENT WILL REMAIN IN EFFECT FOR THE FOLLOWING DAY, AND WILL REMAIN IN EFFECT UNTIL THE ADMINISTRATION CALLS A LOCKUP. DO <u>NOT</u> REPORT TO WORK...

<u>HERE ARE A FEW CHANGES WE EXPECT TO BE BROUGHT ABOUT</u>.

1. AN OPPORTUNITY FOR ALL PAROLE VIOLATORS TO BE AFFORDED A HEARING IN A COURT OF LAW: TO CALL WITNESSES IN THEIR BEHALF: TO CROSS EXAMINE THOSE WITNESSES WHO APPEAR AGAINST THEM: TO BE REPRESENTED BY COUNSEL.

2. COMPLETE ABOLISHMENT OF THE INCREASED PENALTIES FOR NARCOTICS OFFENDERS WITH PRIOR FELONY CONVICTIONS. SEVERAL MEN HERE ARE NOW SERVING ANYWHERE FROM 10 TO 15 YEARS TO LIFE AS A RESULT OF THIS STUPID LAW. ISN'T 5 YEARS TO LIFE SUFFICIENT? THE PENALTY IS NO DETERRENT TO CRIME. THIS HAS BEEN PROVEN TIME AND AGAIN.

3. THAT MORE FAVORABLE CONSIDERATION BE GIVEN TO FIRST OFFENDERS WHEN THEIR MINIMUM TIME IS COMPLETED. TO COMPEL A PERSON TO LINGER IN PRISON CAN ONLY LEAD TO FORMING A HARDENED CRIMINAL. TOO MUCH TIME DESTROYS ANY CONSTRUCTIVE THINGS THE PRISONER HAS ACCOMPLISHED.

4. A DEMAND FOR THE REMOVAL OF ALL EX LAW ENFORCEMENT OFFICERS FROM THE ADULT AUTHORITY, AND THAT THEY BE REPLACED WITH PROFESSORS,

PSYCHOLOGISTS, ETC., WHO ARE MORE FAMILIAR WITH THE CRIMINAL.

5. THE IMMEDIATE REMOVAL OF ALL CHILD SEX OFFENDERS TO MENTAL HOSPITALS WHERE THEY CAN RECEIVE THE HELP NECESSARY TO OVERCOME THEIR ILLNESS.

6. TO COMPEL THE ADULT AUTHORITY TO RECONSIDER ALL CASES WHO APPEARED BEFORE THEM SINCE OCTOBER, 1967 AT THE TIME WHICH THE NEW TIME SCALE WENT INTO EFFECT. ALMOST ALL PRISONERS WHO APPEARED BEFORE THE BOARD SINCE OCTOBER HAVE BEEN DENIED. A GOOD INDICATION THAT YOU WILL DO MORE TIME.

7. DEMANDS FOR BETTER FOOD AND LIVING CONDITIONS WITHIN THE PRISON. APPROXIMATELY $2,600.00 IS APPROPRIATED ANNUALLY FOR YOUR SUPPORT. DID YOU KNOW THAT $14.00 IS APPROPRIATED EACH YEAR JUST SO YOU CAN HAVE A NEW MATTRESS? HOW LONG HAS IT BEEN SINCE YOU'VE HAD ONE? THIS IS JUST <u>ONE</u> ITEM. WE COULDN'T BEGIN TO LIST THEM ALL.

8. COMPLETE REVISION OF THE PRESENT PAY SCALE. PRICES IN THE CANTEEN CONTINUE TO SHOOT SKYWARD. THE DRAW HAS BEEN RAISED TO $30.00 A MONTH. CAN YOU DRAW $30.00 ON YOUR PRESENT PAY?

9. DEMAND THAT A DOCTOR BE <u>AVAILABLE WITHIN THE PRISON</u> AROUND THE CLOCK IN ORDER TO PREVENT <u>UNLAWFUL DEATHS</u> SUCH AS THAT OF WALTER ATKINSON, A-82632, ON NOVEMBER 5, 1964. DIDN'T THINK WE KNEW ABOUT THAT, DID YOU DOCTOR McNAMERA? WANT US TO GIVE YOU A FULL REPORT? HE DIED AS A RESULT OF RESPIRATORY DIFFICULTY, THIS IS TRUE. <u>BUT</u>, ONLY BECAUSE HIS JAWS WERE WIRED TOGETHER FOLLOWING SURGERY, AND HE STRANGLED ON HIS OWN VOMIT. YOU

WERE DRUNK WHEN YOU FINALLY DID SHOW UP, WEREN'T YOU DOCTOR? WE KNOW. WE ALSO HAVE PHOTOSTAT COPIES OF THE COMPLETE RECORDS. WONDER IF JOHN CONLEY, D.D.S., WOULD SUPPORT YOUR CLAIMS? WE WILL SEE SOON ENOUGH.

10. THAT YOUR PAROLE OFFICER BE COMPELLED TO PUT THE APPROVAL OF ANY REQUEST YOU MAKE IN WRITING IN ORDER THAT HE MAY NOT BE PERMITTED TO USE THESE THINGS TO JUSTIFY VIOLATING THE CONDITIONS OF YOUR PAROLE AT HIS OWN WHIM OR CAPRICE.

THESE ARE THE MORE IMPORTANT THINGS WE EXPECT TO ACCOMPLISH AS A RESULT OF OUR MOVEMENT. THERE ARE OTHER ISSUES, SOME MORE IMPORTANT, OTHERS LESS, WHICH WE WILL BRING TO YOU AS SOON AS THE COMPLETE FORMAT HAS BEEN DRAWN...

Let me back up slightly at this point. During the summer of 1967, ML shared a copy of *The Outlaw* with me and explained what they ultimately hoped to accomplish. In addition to major articles dealing with serious issues, the writers always included some trivial things seen as lighthearted to prisoners but embarrassing to staff—things such as a supposedly secret affair a certain guard was having with another guard's wife. The trivia was included to keep the general prisoner readership interested in reading *The Outlaw* and looking forward to the next edition. However, the staff was furious about both the serious *and* lighthearted subjects. Gradually I accumulated quite a collection of *Outlaws* which ML surreptitiously gave to me when I was in the prison.

I became extremely upset with the serious issues raised by *The Outlaw*. I knew that the convicts who produced the paper wanted some of the editions to reach the streets and be brought to the attention of the public. After a few months, the **public** release of *The Outlaw* had yet to occur, and the possibility of it happening did not appear to be promising. Consequently, I asked ML if he would be agreeable to my *anonymously* and *surreptitiously* sharing some copies of *The Outlaw* and discussing the prisoners' concerns with the outside press. He was delighted, but concerned that someone might snitch on me, resulting in my being kicked out of San Quentin. I was willing to take the risk in order to get the public's attention and hopefully have the information reach legislators.

The major San Francisco Bay Area newspapers were reluctant to report about the forthcoming Convict Unity Holiday. However, the *Berkeley Barb*, the popular underground San Francisco Bay Area newspaper—widely distributed and sold on Bay Area streets—was not. At the beginning of January, I approached Jim Schreiber, one of the *Barb*'s best reporters. He agreed to *not* reveal me as the source of the information which I shared with him during a several-hour-long interview. I also gave Jim copies I had made of about forty pages of *The Outlaw*, including the January, 1968 issue quoted above.

Within a few days, the next weekly edition of the *Barb* had the entire front page and both middle pages devoted to Convict Unity Holiday and *The Outlaw*. For weeks, until well after the prisoners' Holiday, the *Barb*'s coverage, with pictures and revealing articles, continued. ML was delighted with the *Barb*'s coverage. He was amused that the *Barb* was regarded as an *underground* newspaper—noting that its address and phone number appear in each edition. He added that *The Outlaw* truly is underground.

The news from the *Barb* immediately generated reaction by younger adults and other people on the streets—those who routinely read the Barb and often were involved in social action. A major demonstration of support for the prisoners by various groups and people was planned for February 15th, outside the main gate of San Quentin. It was a demonstration that had quickly taken on a life of its own.

I approached Daryl Lembke, the San Francisco reporter for the *Los Angeles Times* who did agree to talk with me. In his San Francisco office, I added details to what had been reported in the *Barb* and gave him a couple of copies of *The Outlaw*. He thanked me and assured my confidentiality would be respected. However, somewhat to my disappointment, he said he would *not* immediately report on what I had shared with him—in order to not *create* news. However, he assured me that if Convict Unity Holiday *did* occur, he would write an article about it. Later, after the prisoners' Holiday began, he used my material and wrote what I consider was, by far, the best article by the *non-*

underground press; it appeared in both the *Los Angeles Times* and the *San Francisco Chronicle*.

Administrators tried to keep prisoners from knowing what might occur on the 15th. The *Barb* was forbidden inside, but that didn't stop some staff from bringing copies in. As with *The Outlaw*, if a prisoner was caught with a copy of the *Berkeley Barb*, he would be thrown into "the hole" for 29 days—no questions asked. Prisoners actually were uncertain if a demonstration would occur outside to support them. Even those of us on the outside were not certain *if* or *how large* the demonstration would be. Consequently, from past experiences, many prisoners were reluctant to expect very much.

For me, February 14th, the day *before* Convict Unity Holiday proved to be tremendously interesting and packed with excitement, fear and surprise—which combined to make the day truly unforgettable. The prisoners were cautious, tempering their excitement so they would not be too disappointed if the demonstration fizzled the next day.

During the morning I visited an Anglo prisoner who was the clerk in the hospital pharmacy. He had an interesting prison job—working in the pharmacy. The staff had always been careful to try to have the prisoner in that job be a trustworthy one who would not deal drugs to prisoners. The convicts always had been able to manipulate the prisoner who held that job. Even though this pharmacy clerk was not Chicano, I had been assured that he was trustworthy—convict-like. We talked for a few minutes, and before I left he whispered that he had a copy of the *latest* edition of *The Outlaw* which he would give to me. Very interested in what the latest issue would have to say, I took the single-page issue, folded it a couple of times and slipped it under my belt, inside my pants.

Soon I was leaving through the count gate to go to lunch in the staff snack bar. As soon as I was outside the gate, a custody lieutenant came up and started walking beside me. He said, "The Warden wants to see you." I did a double take, but immediately thought that someone must have said that I intended to "tell it like it is." So, since I had repeatedly practiced how I would explain that comment to satisfy staff curiosity, I was not too worried.

The lieutenant and I went to the Warden's office—a huge room with a giant wooden desk on one end, with rows of stuffed leather chairs extending out from both ends of the desk. Gradually, I became worried as others gathered: Warden Nelson, Associate Warden Administration Park, Associate Warden Custody Wham, the custody Captain, a custody Lieutenant, several guards, and three members of the "Goon Squad" (custody's swat team). By now I was scared, not knowing what all of them were doing there.

Finally, I was told that they had reason to believe I had a copy of *The Outlaw* in my possession. Panicked, my mind raced as I tried to figure out what to say. Next I heard someone say that they believed I was the leak to the *Berkeley Barb* and then ask if that was true. Again, my mind raced as I started to answer, but stopped, not knowing what to say. Then, the next thing I heard was someone say that they would call and have the Marin County District Attorney come out if I didn't immediately cooperate.

Now I knew what to do. I quickly pulled the folded copy of *The Outlaw* out from inside the top of my pants and handed it to them. If I recall correctly they didn't ask about the *Barb* again.

However, that was not the end of things. They had me remove my shoes so they could see if I had some sort of hidden compartment in one of the heels. They demanded to see my wallet; they took all the things out of it—including a miniature address book, which they copied along with other personal papers. Next, on their command, I removed articles of clothing—from suit jacket to pants—all of which they meticulously searched. Finally I ended up standing in front of them, stripped to my shorts with arms outstretched.

They informed me that I never was to be allowed inside the prison again unless I had the written permission of the Warden, two Associate Wardens and the Captain. Then they told me to get dressed and go to my car—accompanied by the three members of the goon squad who would search my car—and then leave for the last time, "unless we can get you back in here with a number behind your name."

Going to my car, I thought of stories I had heard. I feared that the goon squad might "plant" evidence in order to arrest me. I tried to watch all three, attempting to be certain that they did not "find" something—something that had not been there before.

To say I breathed a gigantic sigh of relief as I drove out through the prison gates for the last time is a gross understatement. My mind raced. I was thankful that I had not been arrested. However, I didn't know if I might have committed some technical crime that would end up allowing CDC or San Quentin authorities to have me arrested. I was certain that I did *not* want to end up in prison with a number behind my name as had been noted earlier when I was kicked out.

That evening I met with a few people who knew what I had been doing regarding *The Outlaw* and the *Barb*. They shared my concern about what my legal status was. I tried, but failed to get a call through to a young attorney they knew for advice. I was frightened, unsure where I legally stood. Later, one individual came into the room and gave me a yellow pin with black lettering that read: "EVEN PARANOIDS HAVE REAL ENEMIES." He told me I needed it more than he did. That night turned out to be quite restless for me, with very little sleep.

Convict Unity Holiday

The next morning, February 15, 1968, well before the beginning of any demonstration outside of San Quentin in support of prisoners and their Convict Unity Holiday, I called an older, well-established attorney in Oakland who was recommended by my brother-in-law. The attorney calmly asked me to relate what had happened. Finally, he assured me that I had done nothing illegal. However, he *did* suggest that I not publicly admit that I had been the leak to the *Berkeley Barb*—at least not for awhile.

I had not planned things this way. I did not intend to get kicked out of San Quentin and have my research inside terminated. However, *I suddenly was free to openly talk in public!*

Originally, *The Outlaw* had successfully served as the prisoners' covert spokesman. Later those efforts were coupled with my confidential contacts with the *Berkeley Barb* and its publicity of the prisoners' Convict Unity Holiday. Now, after my being kicked out of San Quentin the preceding day, I could publicly be a person who knew details of the previously hidden reality inside. Prison administrators, from San Quentin to the top ones in Sacramento, were furious that the hidden, often embarrassing reality inside was no longer under their control. I would continue to be able to break through CDC's almost absolute power to control the flow of information from within prison and openly share my knowledge to enlighten outsiders and legislators. I was still shaken from the traumatic events of the preceding day, but delighted with my new freedom. (My earlier section about CDC's secrecy and absolute power is pertinent here.)

Inside the prison, staff tried to thwart the strike by starting *all* normal prisoner activities an hour early. Still, about 20 percent of the almost 4,000 prisoners went on strike. However, even those prisoners who did *not* strike returned to their cells an hour early. So, having started an hour early, *almost all prisoners were in their cells before 3:00* for the daily count of all prisoners (on a normal day this would occur between 4:00 and 4:30).

Outside the main gate of the prison, roughly 400 to 500 supporters of the prisoners' Holiday gradually gathered. They had been drawn by the reports in the *Barb* and elsewhere that The Grateful Dead and The Phoenix were going to play for the prisoners and demonstrators, thus adding their support to the prisoners' cause.

The throng filled more than the narrow street leading to the prison gate. About a hundred yards east of the main gate, a small peninsula juts southeast into the northern end of the San Francisco Bay for a few hundred yards. The north*east* side of the peninsula leads to the start of the Richmond-San Rafael Bridge. The south*west* side is grassy and clear of trees and brush for a couple hundred yards. There, the part of the throng of supporters on the peninsula had a clear view across a small inlet of the bay to the prison—southwest they could see the prison, particularly the stark, imposing East block.

Since the musicians were night people, they were not early risers. Consequently, they arrived well after noon. First a huge truck, pulling a very long flat trailer, slowly edged its way through the crowd and made its way to the end of the cleared area on the small peninsula. Soon, the giant black-shrouded load was uncovered, revealing the Grateful Dead's mammoth speakers and sound equipment. The speakers were positioned so their full volume would blast a few hundred yards across the water to the East block. By the time the musicians arrived, set things up, and were ready to play, *all* the prisoners in east-facing cells in East block were in their cells, standing at their bars, waiting for the daily count to begin.

Suddenly the concert began! Even though the prisoners had not yet known if they had support on the outside, now they knew! Their shouts of thanks and approval from inside were drowned out by the music of the Grateful Dead and The Phoenix. The volume of the bands was so loud that *all the prisoners in all four cell blocks heard*! The rumors of outside support had been true!

With my one-year-old daughter on my shoulders and my wife and two-year-old son beside me, I joined an outside chorus of shouts of approval by the throng of supporters surrounding us.

Soon, when my family and I were near the gate, a guard sergeant I had frequently seen inside, who was filming the crowd, yelled some forgettable obscenity at me, and then swore at my wife as he flipped her the finger.

Later, when I was near the gate, I observed through the bars that a San Francisco CBS TV reporter and cameraman were interviewing Mr. Park, the Associate Warden Administration, who was about 100 yards from me—inside the gate. Park was standing on the lawn, in front of the attractively-landscaped Administration Building as a backdrop. (This and other staff buildings were outside the actual prison walls.) The interview continued for about a half hour or more. I realized that the reporter was probably getting the administration's *very long, spoon-fed version* of what the administration wanted the public to know about the strike inside.

Since I had been approached by the TV crew as it was arriving—apparently someone had revealed that I was the person who had leaked the prisoners' information to the *Barb*—I had been forewarned. Just in case I would face the TV camera, I thought about what I might say.

Soon the TV reporter and cameraman were outside the gate, interviewing me. Knowing that brief statements were all that were ever shown on newscasts, I quickly noted six points, briefly explaining each. I prefaced two of those points with, "Associate Warden Park probably will tell you..." Immediately I went on to add what *I thought Park might say*, briefly following with *my explanation* of the point.

That night, the CBS news report included almost nothing from the half-hour interview with Park. However, all six brief points that I related were shown. I was particularly pleased when the two times I prefaced points and followed with what *I thought* Park would probably say were immediately followed by a clip of Park actually saying almost exactly what I had thought he might say. Then, after each of those two times, the TV switched back to my brief explanations of the other points which were strikingly different from what Park had said or purposely omitted. I was elated! I caught Park trying to manipulate the public by telling lies on camera!

As I noted earlier, when I confidentially met with Darrel Lembke , the San Francisco reporter for the *Los Angeles Times*, he had assured me that *if* Convict Unity Holiday *did* occur, he would use the material I provided him and write an article about it. The day after Convict Unity Holiday began, he wrote what I consider was, by far, the best article published in the *non*-underground press. It was the *only* such article to appear in any of the "legitimate" presses. No paper other than the *Barb* and the *Los Angeles Times* had been privy to the detailed information I was able to provide. Lembke's article appeared in both the *Los Angeles Times* and the *San Francisco Chronicle*. I was delighted that my efforts paid off.

On the Sunday following Convict Unity Holiday, I was the single guest on "Next Question," the San Francisco CBS TV's Sunday news interview program. I was interviewed by a small panel of the station's top newscasters. Unfortunately, they were unacquainted with the reality behind the walls of San Quentin and with the issues behind Convict Unity Holiday. Beyond a few general questions, the panel seemed to draw a blank—few specific questions were asked. Consequently I ended up giving an informative talk for the better part of the hour while the newscasters listened.

Within days, I was interviewed by a reporter from radio station KPFA—listener-supported and located in Berkeley. Most people who worked at the station had read the *Berkeley Barb* and were familiar with its earlier articles about Convict Unity Holiday. I feel the hour-long interview was much better than the interview on "Next Question." The reporter knew enough about the prison and the issues involved in the prisoners' Holiday that he was able to ask excellent questions.

Much later, I was not surprised by information I learned about the prisoner who was the pharmacy clerk who surreptitiously gave me the *latest* copy of *The Outlaw* on the day that I was kicked out. Apparently this Anglo, "convict-like" prisoner who had been trusted by true convicts, had been rewarded by administrators for cooperating in setting me up. Almost immediately he had been transferred to another prison (for his own protection from convicts who quickly learned of the setup). Soon he was paroled from the other prison—his reward.

MY NEW FREEDOM

After abruptly being ejected from San Quentin, I found myself no longer under the constraints that had initially been imposed on me by administrators—to control what I could and could not publicly disclose. True, I no longer was allowed inside the prison, so that part of my research had ended. However, my new freedom to publicly reveal what administrators—from San Quentin to CDC in Sacramento—had effectively concealed from public knowledge was exciting and rewarding. For too long I had been frustrated and frequently angered by the secret and sometimes illegal abuses of the ideals underlying the prison and parole system by the very people who were hired to carry out and manage the ideals of the Department of *Corrections*.

I considered my situation. I was a US Army veteran and a mature, law-abiding graduate student from the University of California, Berkeley, with a wife and two young children. I had been conducting legitimate doctoral research among Chicano prisoners.

As cultural anthropologists typically do almost anywhere in the world—from the warlike natives of New Guinea, to the peaceful Bushmen of the Kalahari Desert, to the Mennonites in the U.S.—I had successfully learned a quite different subculture that was in conflict with but definitely a part of the much larger U.S. culture. Anthropologists have often studied cultures in conflict and must try to avoid condemning members in one or the other of two intensely conflicting cultures. Being from the larger U.S. culture, I had strong moral values—a deep sense of what is right and wrong, and how people should and should not be treated. To meet this challenge as anthropologists are expected to do, I understood, but did *not* condemn the prisoners and their often illegal or rule-breaking subcultural practices. I also suspended judgment of what crimes a prisoner may have committed to put him in prison, since he was being punished in accord with the laws of the larger U.S. culture.

Even though I did not condemn the prisoners for their *normal* subcultural behavior, I was morally outraged by what I perceived as gross, abnormal abuse of prisoners and a supposedly ideal prison system by *some* of the prison higher-ranking staff and administrators who pretended to be of high or superior moral character. I intensely felt I must take action on behalf of the prisoners—who had long-been relatively powerless to bring about legitimate legal change on their own behalf.

Therefore, no longer constrained by San Quentin administrators, I was determined to be a uniquely knowledgeable spokesman for prisoners—to attempt to bring about legitimate changes in a prison system that was far from ideal. I hoped that those changes would emanate from the actions of a newly-enlightened California State legislature.

At that time, I never imagined what others—from San Quentin staff and administrators to the FBI—would do to try to "set me up" or entice me to illegally do something I had never imagined doing that would result in my arrest and conviction for a felony, or do something that possibly might result in my getting killed. Their efforts, which I will gradually recount in the following pages, lasted for nearly 29 years. Those efforts began in February, 1968 when a San Quentin counselor unsuccessfully tried to set me up to commit a felony. The last time started in November, 1996 when a Law Clerk from the Federal Public Defenders Office in Los Angeles unsuccessfully tried to get me to give testimony and/or advice in a federal case against 13 members of the Mexican Mafia—12 were convicted of conspiracy and murder in 1997.

POLITICAL EFFORTS IN SACRAMENTO

Within a week after Convict Unity Holiday, I was in Sacramento to talk with a key Assemblyman who had a deep interest in prisons. Craig Biddle, Chairman of the California State Assembly Criminal Procedure

Committee, had heard of me through media reports about Convict Unity Holiday. He wanted to talk with me. Our long conversation resulted in his asking me to come to Sacramento again to give testimony at hearings his committee was going to soon hold concerning California prisons. I was pleased to agree.

Biddle suggested that I talk with Assemblyman John Vasconcellos, who also had a definite interest in prisons. Later, when I entered his office, on the top of his neat, nearly-empty desk was a stack of the recent *Berkeley Barb*s that dealt with Convict Unity Holiday. During our conversation, Vasconcellos agreed with Biddle that my testimony in front of the Criminal Procedure Committee would be very useful for members of the committee.

The testimony given by me and many others from throughout the state resulted in more prison reform bills being *introduced* in the California State Assembly in 1968 than ever before in history. Unfortunately, most of those bills failed to pass and become law.

However, Convict Unity Holiday did lead to a series of communications between the prisoners and Biddle. One year later, in February, 1969, the Criminal Procedure Committee held hearings at San Quentin about abusive practices of the Adult Authority. In spite of the Warden Nelson's forbidding, a prisoner-prepared report titled "A Convict Report on the Major Grievances of the Prison Population with Suggested Solutions" was presented to the members of the committee. The convict-prepared report contained a list of twelve legitimate objections to abusive practices routinely employed by the Adult Authority. The entire convict report is printed in Robert Minton's 1971 book, *Inside Prison American Style*. Regrettably, little of significance materialized from the prisoner-Committee hearings.

SOCIAL PRESSURE FOR CHANGE IN SACRAMENTO

Almost immediately after giving testimony in Sacramento, I realized that significant, legitimate changes in the firmly-entrenched prison system probably would never occur if politicians *alone* were expected to successfully pass laws that would bring about those changes. Consequently, I turned my efforts to additional ways to inform and educate the public about the less-than-ideal prison system. Then, hopefully—through the influence of the general public, community leaders, educators, students and social movements such as the Chicano movement—additional pressure might compel legislators to make desirable changes in the prison system.

CCRC, LUCHA and *CRI*

Soon after giving testimony to the Criminal Procedure Committee, I talked with John Irwin, a college researcher, about what we might do to further push legislators into action. John and I had known each other from when he and his wife had been customers at the San Francisco meat market where I cut meat part- and full-time while I was a graduate student at UC Berkeley. Soon after I began my research at San Quentin, I was pleasantly surprised to discover that John was conducting interviews with a few selected prisoners in the education building. John's movement inside the prison was limited to only the education building at certain times each week. We talked about how my research methods and my focus on Chicano prisoners differed from his limited interviewing method. John would later publish *The Felon* in 1970. His book was excellent, but quite different from the holistic description of the prisoners' own culture that I would later publish in *Chicano Prisoners* in 1974.

Earlier in this memoir, when treating the so-called race riots of 1967, I noted how the education department attempted to spend unused treatment funds by offering a special evening class, with *three* instructors teaching a seminar-style class to a small number of select prisoners. I refused to become involved and accept any money from the prison, but John became one of the three instructors.

Soon after giving my testimony to the Criminal Procedure Committee in Sacramento, John and I formed and became the founding officers of Citizens Committee for Reform in Corrections (CCRC). Bernie Hutner, a Berkeley attorney, became the secretary of our organization. Richard Corn, a criminology professor at UC Berkeley actively participated in many ways. Initially focusing our efforts in Northern California we contacted many people—educating them and pushing them in many ways to take action to bring about change in the prison system. I attended several meetings of criminology classes and seminars Dick Corn was conducting—sharing information from my research with his students.

Bernie Hutner, a member of the Berkeley-Albany Bar Association, invited me to be the speaker at one of the Associations' monthly luncheon meetings. I pulled no punches in my talk—sharing things that had been hidden from outsiders and were embarrassing for San Quentin administrators and CDC. At the end of my hour-long talk, one of the attorneys excitedly told Bernie that the wife of a Berkeley policeman had been in the back of the room and had surreptitiously taped my talk. Bernie, a giant of a man, was furious. He demanded the tape. The woman refused. But when Bernie towered over her and almost yelled at her with his booming voice, the woman reluctantly took the tape from her recorder and gave it to Bernie. Later, Bernie and I played the tape. The first hour of my talk was *not* on the tape. Only the last couple of questions and my replies at the end of my talk were on *this* tape. She had run out of time on her first tape and switched to a second tape for the last couple questions. All we had was the second tape. Bernie and I were furious! It was obvious to us that the hour-long tape probably was going to Warden Nelson at San Quentin.

A month later, Bernie related what occurred at the next monthly meeting. Warden (Big Red) Nelson was the guest speaker. Apparently Nelson ranted on about how wrong and vicious I was. I can't recall all the details, but I do vividly remember Bernie relating that Warden Nelson called me a *fascist warmonger!* I laughed out loud at the absurdity of his choice of terms—they made no sense at all. I guessed that it was the worst thing he could come up with at that moment. This, by the way, came from the mouth of Big Red, the man who—a few months earlier, on February 14th, 1968—had threatened to have me back in San Quentin with a number behind my name. I guess—since I had publicly embarrassed him in many ways—the fascist warmonger remark was his way to angrily, unthinkingly lash out at and discredit me. By the way, I never have had any pity for Big Red.

Other examples of CCRC efforts in Northern California in 1968 and 1969 involved a Law Professor at U.C. Berkeley who interviewed me about San Quentin and CDC, with particular emphasis on the Adult

Authority; he had me sign a document giving him legal permission to use my comments in a section of a two-inch-thick legal volume he was updating. In addition, I gave talks to Rotary and other service organizations in the San Francisco East Bay Area—Berkeley, Albany, Hayward and Oakland.

While the above-noted activities were taking place in Northern California, I was in frequent contact with a close friend, Ed Aguirre, an ex-convict friend from San Quentin who had been released from prison before I was kicked out. He was currently living in the East Los Angeles area of Southern California. Before I actually entered San Quentin for the first time, an administrator at the prison suggested it might be useful for me to visit a CDC Halfway House on Breed Street in the East Los Angeles area. He felt I would gain insight into what I might encounter when I actually started my research inside the prison. I don't recall learning much about prisons during that visit. However, I did meet and talk with one resident at the Halfway House, Archie Aguirre. He suggested I talk with Ed Aguirre, his brother, who was in San Quentin at that time. I followed his advice. It turned out that Ed was a very intelligent, influential Chicano convict. We hit it off well—soon becoming close friends. He was the one who suggested I talk with certain Chicano convicts. Thus, as I noted much earlier, Ed was my personal introduction to many of his convict friends. I soon realized he personally was responsible for the depth of my rapport with Chicano convicts—a rapport that I established quite rapidly thanks to Ed.

Being in frequent contact, Ed Aguirre and I discussed details about the activities of CCRC. Ed was concerned with the plight of so many Chicanos—from narcotic addiction to an abusive prison system. Many of them lived in the greater Los Angeles area. He decided his primary focus would be on Southern California. Soon Ed was the driving force behind the formation of LUCHA (The League of United Citizens to Help Addicts). The primary motive of LUCHA was that they, as ex-narcotics addicts and as a self-help group, identified with the community geographically, ethnically and psychologically. They stood ready to become involved with the total community.

As one spokesman said, "We hope to structure a consensus approach, so that churches, labor unions, community service agencies and organizations, along with student groups and interested and active community residents will appreciate the practicality and effectiveness of working in unity with representatives of the 'weed-roots' segment of our barrio life."

Another spokesman stated, "We're providing the community with an image not ordinarily associated with persons who have a history of drug addiction and anti-social conduct. Our feeling is that now that we're 'Clean,' our 'Cleanness' must be invested in efforts of a constructive and serving nature; after all, our past addiction is but an extreme expression of what relatively stable people experience in their everyday life. When one thinks in terms of what personal frustration, self-rejection, and self-assumed or imposed feeling of inferiority can do to people in general, one can understand the logic of my statement."

In its tireless work to reach its extensive goals LUCHA did many diverse things. Let me note a few of those. LUCHA joined LA RAZA NUEVA, a group of Chicanos devoted to attaining justice for Chicanos *now*. LUCHA participated in the "Viva Kennedy" campaign. LUCHA worked and demonstrated for the release and acquittal of The Chicano 13 who had been arrested and jailed in Los Angeles for conspiracy to better the education in barrio schools.

LUCHA aligned itself with the United Farm Workers in their struggle for unionism. I recall joining Ed Aguirre and a couple of Chicanos in one car. We joined two other cars full of Chicanos as we drove from Los Angeles to Delano, California. Our trip was to meet with Cesar Chavez and show our support for his efforts to unionize Chicano farm workers.

LUCHA arranged a meeting at Lincoln High School auditorium, where Ray Procunier, the Director of California Department of Corrections was the guest speaker. He was to answer questions the Chicano community had about San Quentin and CDC. Ed had me come as a member of audience since I knew the prison system so well and was not constrained in my questions as parolees were. After Procunier's introductory statements, and after a few questions were asked by other members of the audience, I stood up to ask a question. I could immediately tell by the look on Ray's face that he was *not* pleased with my presence This was not the first time Ray and I had faced off in public. He had learned from my testimony in Sacramento that I knew the prison system and its abuses well enough to ask straightforward, often embarrassing questions.

LUCHA helped organize a Black-Brown motorcade to support the 1973 election of Los Angeles Mayor Bradley, the first African-American mayor of a major U.S. city. The motorcade, with many convertibles, horns blowing and festively-dressed women spent the afternoon winding its way back and forth through the Black ghettos and Chicano barrios. That evening, my wife and I (the only Anglos present) attended the very noisy, crowded, festive party at Ed Aguirre's home. The motorcade had been quite successful.

A particularly interesting effort by LUCHA was the setting up of "safe houses" to aid addicts in their desire to withdraw (dry out) from addiction. Most LUCHA activities were legal but these *secret* safe houses were not sanctioned by parole authorities and skirted the law.

Upper class addicts can afford to pay to dry out from addiction. They can go to some expensive private retreat and pay a lot of money to be pampered and treated by licensed professionals. However, most Chicanos lack the resources to get *that* kind of treatment. True, there are some free governmental programs to help addicts withdraw, but the treatment is far different. And, an addict would have to admit to drug use—which could result in parole violation if on parole, or perhaps court and possibly prison if no previous drug-use record existed.

With LUCHA's *secret* safe houses, the Chicano addicts—with or without a criminal record—would not have to go to authorities and admit addiction in order to receive the less than superior governmental withdrawal help. Instead, those who wanted help could go to a safe house where those who helped the addicts through the hell of withdrawal were Chicano ex-addicts who had quite real personal knowledge of the process—not licensed professionals. LUCHA's safe houses may have been illegal, *but* they were extremely successful.

Committee for the Rights of the Imprisoned (CRI) was a direct outgrowth of CCRC, LUCHA and my routine involvement with Ed Aguirre and Bernie Hutner. Concerned about having free, long-term, excellent legal representation for Chicanos—something often lacking when they used the services of public defenders and other existing free services—we started CRI. Our goal was to set up legal offices in both the Los Angeles and San Francisco areas. We wanted to hire full-time attorneys to provide legal representation for needy Chicanos for at least two years—or more if funding continued beyond two years. We intended to apply for grants from a variety of sources.

Bernie Hutner set CRI up as a non-profit corporation. He was Secretary and I was President. Ed Aguirre had an excellent resource in the Los Angeles area who had a history of considerable success in obtaining grants from a variety of sources. The woman was not daunted that the probable total grant to accomplish what we planned could possibly reach up to a million dollars. After, a few years of extensive efforts to fund CRI, we realized that we would not be able to fund and accomplish CRI's goals. Bernie and I dropped our active participation, but Ed continued to use CRI to accomplish lesser goals in the Los Angeles area.

I'd like to make a few additional, quite personal comments about Ed Aguirre. Our friendship and mutual respect became deep-felt. It lasted for years after we first met in San Quentin in June, 1966. In prison, he often was supportive of Chicano self-help efforts, such as EMPLEO. Later, on the streets, he persistently and tirelessly pursued similar goals, such as LUCHA and CRI. At the drop of a hat we would drive the length of the state to visit or help each other. Ed frequently visited our home, becoming "Uncle Ed" to my son and daughter. My wife and I visited Ed and his girlfriend at his home in Los Angeles, and they joined us several times for dinner at our place. We both recognized—each in the other—a sincere desire to bring about legitimate, positive changes in society, with an deep emphasis on helping Chicanos and changing the abusive prison system.

In late spring, 1969, I finally reached a financial crisis. I had maximized my educational loans and needed to work full-time to support my family. Consequently, I took a leave of absence from the doctoral program in anthropology at U.C. Davis. I rather frantically searched for a teaching position and succeeding in securing a position at Cabrillo College, starting Fall, 1969

College professor,
1969-1993

Cabrillo College

Cabrillo College is located in Aptos California, near Santa Cruz. I began teaching cultural and physical anthropology classes in the fall of 1969. Compared to Berkeley, Aptos was rather conservative, with a large, relatively complacent middle class population. There was little of the excitement of social movements that had been manifest in Berkeley. However, that soon would change with the impact of the war in Vietnam and the spread of social protest in California to campuses such as U.C. Santa Cruz.

In my cultural anthropology classes, for the first time, I could devote a section of my lectures to my research among Chicano Prisoners in San Quentin. My students were fascinated. Instead of learning about a culture or sub-culture by reading an ethnography, now they had an anthropologist who actually did the research in front of them. They could ask me any questions about the prison that came to their minds. They enjoyed the experience, as did I. In my lectures, I pulled no punches about how the *real* prisoner culture differed from the ideal prison system portrayed to the public by prison administrators and CDC.

It was an enjoyable challenge to teach cultural and physical anthropology classes for the first time. However, it took a few months before I began to sense subtle things that began occurring—things that suggested the degree to which the conservative elements in the community exercised considerable control over activities in the Santa Cruz-Aptos area.

For example, when I lived in Berkeley, I routinely bought the *Berkeley Barb* and the *Black Panther*—both papers were widely hawked by young people on the streets in Berkeley. I did so because, as an anthropologist, I wanted to keep informed of the latest social issues. Since those two papers were not readily available when I moved to Aptos, I subscribed and had them mailed to me. One day, my younger, bearded mailman, as if he was telling me a secret, almost whispered to me, "You know, you're the only person in this entire mailing district that subscribes to the Black Panther." I replied that the paper comes in a brown wrapper with no identifying return address. I asked how he knew. His response was, "Oh, they know." His interaction that day was almost like kindred spirits sharing secrets. I pondered, how and why did "they" get that information?

During the Christmas holidays, I painted a large, red and green Peace Symbol on one front window of our home and a large heart with "PEACE" written across it on another. One evening a group of neighbors were caroling—stopping and walking up near the door of each home to sing. We expected to open our door and greet them when they came to our home. However, they did not stop at our place. A curious disappointment for my family.

In the spring semester, 1970, Larry, a slightly older student enrolled in one of my cultural anthropology classes. He went out of his way to find occasions outside of class to talk with me. In our conversations, he revealed bits and pieces about himself that never really held together too well. He claimed he had lived in the area, served in the military at some time in some capacity and parked in the faculty parking lot because of some sort of disability which was not obvious. I became suspicious, wondering if he was an undercover agent spying on me for some governmental agency.

Soon, something quite strange occurred. A middle-aged couple I had met and talked with about my research in San Quentin invited my wife and me to have dinner with them. They lived in a somewhat remote forested area on a back road in the Santa Cruz mountains. A few days before our visit, I called them to get directions to their place. Shortly after my wife and I arrived, we were surprised when Larry drove up and quite awkwardly introduced himself to the couple. Then he told me some unintelligible reason why he was there. I don't think the couple could make sense out of Larry's unexpected appearance, but they politely invited him to stay. The red flags were flying! This confirmed my earlier suspicions that Larry was some sort of undercover agent— one who was not too adept though. I did *not* reveal my discovery to him, but I was careful in my dealings with him after that evening. And, he did continue showing up by *just happening to be somewhere I was.*

Lightning struck across the United States! In early May, 1970, the sudden discovery and disclosure by the media of what previously had been the secret bombing of Cambodia by the U.S. created a firestorm of protest. At Cabrillo College, I first heard the news as I arrived for my early morning class. A whirlwind of activity immediately began. Within an hour I was on a student-faculty picket line—protesting the bombing of Cambodia and the Vietnam War. All classes were canceled. An umbrella organization of students—including all groups and students interested in protesting—was soon formed. I was asked to be the faculty advisor of the umbrella organization; I accepted.

(PLEASE NOTE: Some individuals and groups in the influential conservative elements of the Santa Cruz-Aptos area did *not* appreciate or support the war protests. They supported President Nixon and his war in Vietnam. Please keep this in mind. I will refer to them later.)

The faculty was outraged and took immediate action, placing a statement of protest in both the local papers—the *Santa Cruz Sentinel* and *Watsonville Register-Pajaronian*—on May 7, 1970.

"We, the undersigned faculty members of Cabrillo College, deplore the increased involvement of the United States in southeast Asia, the sending of American troops into Cambodia, and the resumption of bombing in North Vietnam.

We feel a sense of outrage at the wholesale destruction of human life there.

We strongly object to President Nixon's directing the invasion of a neutral country without Congressional approval.

We believe that domestic problems are being neglected in order that our military commitments be maintained or expanded.

We protest President Nixon's latest decision concerning this government's posture in Indochina."

A total of 75 faculty members signed the statement. When I signed, I did not even think about the fact that I had *not* been granted tenure and the potential consequences of signing the statement.

An anti-war rally took place in the plaza in front of the post office in Santa Cruz. For over two hours the 1,000 attending listened to the impassioned pleas of speakers from the community to strike for peace. The following day, both local papers had articles about the rally and a total of 11 pictures. I was quite recognizable in a picture that appeared in both papers. I was holding a pole: At the top was a bleached human skull without the mandible. Below that was foot-long black shroud. Below, at the bottom was a vertical, black-lettered sign that on both sides simply said S T O P. The caption below the picture in both newspapers simply stated, "one man's silent but visual protest."

Continued pressure from students in the newly-formed umbrella student protest organization and from faculty resulted in extreme changes in classes, schedules and grades for that spring semester. Some classes met less frequently or not at all, assignments were changed to allow students time for planning protest efforts, class attendance was relaxed or non-existent, some grades were virtually given away, and many other things occurred that probably gave Cabrillo College administrators nightmares. Some faculty complained that the relaxing or abandonment of standards merely gave many students more time to spend at the beach.

Also in May, 1970, I met with SH, an older Black student who was actively involved in the Black movement and most recently in the anti-war rally against the bombing of Cambodia and the war in Vietnam. Without being invited, Larry showed up at her home this particular day. As the three of us discussed the recent protests against the war and additional ways that peaceful protests could be made against the war, out of the blue, Larry abruptly asked us, "Do you have any connections to people who could help make bombs?" SH and I were shocked! Larry's question was far removed from the legal, legitimate protests we had been discussing. SH and I glanced at each other and rolled our eyes in disbelief. Soon, after Larry left, SH and I shared our belief about Larry—agreeing that his bomb question confirmed in our minds that he was in fact an *agent provocateur!* He was to be avoided whenever possible.

In late spring of 1970, my wife and I started house hunting since our one-year rental lease on our subdivision home was to end in July. We finally found a fabulous place in a redwood canyon several miles east of the college. With a rustic home overlooking the meeting of two creeks, four acres forested with redwoods, the nearest neighbor over a quarter mile away, and almost no traffic on the narrow, twisting road, we fell in love with it. The owner of the property did not want to use the usual sale through a mortgage company with transfer of deed of ownership etcetera. Instead, on the advice and with the help of our realtor, we purchased the home using a contract of sale.

In my second year at Cabrillo College, I proposed conducting a community seminar which was to be called "Convicts, Corrections and the Community" (CCC). John Irwin and I would moderate a panel of experts. A parole officer and a prison guard would represent CDC. A CDC-selected prisoner (not my choice and probably not a convict) would be brought by the guard from Soledad Prison. Ed Aguirre, John Irwin and I would represent the convicts. The administrative and faculty support and feedback from the community was considerable. CCC was to be held in the evening in the college auditorium and was publicized in may ways throughout the community.

On the day before CCC, I received a call from the assistant to Ray Procunier, the Director of CDC. Procunier's assistant informed me that *CDC was not going to allow any of its people to participate!*

I couldn't believe what I had heard. The assistant repeated his statement and elaborated—the parole agent from the San Jose parole office, and the guard and prisoner from Soledad Prison would **NOT** attend! He concluded by adding, *"Procunier doesn't want our people being ripped apart by you."*

I immediately talked with Bob Swenson, Cabrillo's President. He too was dumbfounded. He wondered if we should cancel the program. I assured him that we should go ahead with the community seminar and openly announce at the beginning what CDC had done. CCC proved to be interesting, educational and at times exciting for the community. It filled the auditorium. The favorable feedback was significant.

In 1971, near the beginning of the spring semester, I had reached a financial crisis, so I approached the college credit union for a personal loan. Informed that I did not qualify for the loan I wanted and would need a co-signer, I approached Gene Wright, an older, well-established professor of criminal studies. Gene and I had talked extensively about my research, and I spoke with a couple of his classes. He was a member of Cabrillo's Community Services Committee and had actively supported my giving CCC. Gene gladly co-signed for me.

Soon, all hell broke loose!
I was told I would not be rehired for the 1971-72 school year!

I panicked! *Publicly*, the college administrators claimed that I did not meet their instructional standards. Since my student evaluations had been excellent, I didn't understand their decision. Immediately I talked with Gene Wright. Since I already had been informed of the decision, he—in strictest confidence revealed the *real* reason behind the administration's decision to essentially *fire* me.

Gene, being one of the senior professors was a member of the college personnel committee. He had been sworn to secrecy to not reveal what actually was the reason for firing me. Also, he was not to reveal the decision to anyone before it was made public. Gene knew of the decision to fire me *before* I applied for a loan from the credit union. Being sworn to secrecy, he could not reveal the administration's decision to me. However, as a friend and colleague, he co-signed for me—confident that I would repay the loan. When I pressed him for more information regarding why I was fired, he pointed out that my research, which was critical of CDC, and my protest against the Vietnam War were the real reasons for firing me. He also told me that one of the most conservative administrators excitedly warned the other personnel committee members, "Davidson's a raving maniac of a revolutionary who dares criticize California Department of Corrections and protest the war in Vietnam!" Since I had no tenure, there was no way I could contest the college administrators' decision—they would never publicly reveal their real reason for firing me.

I urgently needed to find another teaching position. I quickly prepared three different professional vitae for Universities, Colleges and Community Colleges. I sent the appropriate vita to most of those institutions on the west coast—over 100 vitae sent.

Soon I got a call for me to come for an interview. After the interview, I was quite pleased. I sensed that things had gone quite well—that I may have landed a job. Then, about four days later, I received a phone call from the principal person who had conducted the interview. He said, "I'm sorry Mr. Davidson. We've already hired someone for that position."

That scenario was repeated, occurring a total of eleven times! I had traveled the state for interviews, from San Diego to Crescent City. When I received the twelfth call, I traveled to El Camino College in Torrance, California. Again, the interview went well. About four days later I received a call from the Dean who had interviewed me. Expecting the worst, I was astonished. They wanted me to begin teaching classes in September!

During my job-searching, I felt certain that the FBI or some governmental agency had my phone tapped. Learning of eleven of my interviews, agents obviously called each time to discourage each place from hiring me. Fortunately, I guess that someone made a mistake or forgot to make a call the twelfth time.

I was and still am furious that agents from one or more of those governmental agencies had secretly tried to destroy me—and my family—financially! I do understand the need for the FBI in a free society. However, I sincerely believe they went beyond reasonable limits they should follow. I will never forget!

While my job search was taking place, I had to resolve another major issue. What was I to do regarding the Contract of Sale I had signed during the summer to purchase our mountain home? The owner of the house and Contract of Sale refused to let me out of the agreement. I argued that I had done a great deal to improve the landscaping and other things after my family and I moved in; those improvements would remain with the property. The owner would not budge. Finally

I contacted William Locke-Paddon, a Watsonville attorney, to see if he could help me extricate myself from the Contract of Sale. So, for months, the routine payments no longer went to the owner. Instead they went to a trust fund where they accumulated. Finally the owner— missing a significant amount of income—capitulated, let me off the hook and took his money.

So, we were able to spend the 4th of July moving from our rustic, creek-side mountain home to a small tract home in Redondo Beach.

EL CAMINO COLLEGE

At El Camino College in the fall of 1971, no one ever asked, and I was careful to not breathe a word to anyone at the college, about the circumstances surrounding my being fired from Cabrillo College. From the college administration's silence on the subject, I initially assumed and was pleased that the FBI or some other agency did not directly contact administrators.

Before long however, I suspected that a young couple, Robe and Shirley—two students in their mid-twenties who had enrolled in one of my cultural anthropology classes—were two undercover agents. They were quite friendly with me and frequently talked with me outside of class. They (particularly Robe) seemed to be overly-fascinated with my research and my continuing activities with the Chicano movement. They claimed to have been going steady for over a year.

I became suspicious of the absence of subtle things. The two were pleasant to each other, but never did I see the slightest hint of the love and gestures of close friendship that normally are manifest in a long-standing, steady relationship. I became wary of the two—particularly Robe. He seemed to push exceptionally hard for information about my current activities.

Months later, when talking with Robe, I described some difficulties I was having with an individual in the Chicano movement who was being unreasonable. Before I could explain what I intended to legally do to get the individual to back off, Robe whispered an unexpected, startling offer to me. He told me that if I needed to get rid of the guy, *he had connections to get the guy killed for me!* All I had to do was let Robe know who the guy was!

It was a challenge to *not* show my shock. I continued to talk with Robe and Shirley from time to time for a couple of years or more. However, I was extremely guarded in my interaction. I did *not* reveal to Robe and Shirley that I knew they were undercover agent provocateurs—willing to provoke me into doing something I had never imagined doing. I believed that if I told them what I really thought about them, they would cut off communication some way and probably be replaced by some other undercover agent who would try to do a better job.

Earlier, while at Cabrillo College, the book representative for Holt, Rinehart and Winston talked with me about my research in San Quentin. He conveyed what he learned to Dave Boynton, Editor-in-chief, College Department at Holt. Dave wrote to me in March, 1971, quite interested in my proposed ethnography about San Quentin. Unfortunately, my being fired from Cabrillo at that time took all of my time and effort, so a hiatus occurred until I began teaching at El Camino. Dave and I resumed communication in September, 1971, when Dave wrote, "There is no question but that we shall want to publish your book."

Many letters and phone calls between Dave and me, as well Dave's visit to me at my home in Redondo Beach, took place until publication of *Chicano Prisoners* in 1974. I was aware of the current social significance of my research—that it could be used to bring about timely, needed legitimate changes—so I arranged to immediately use my material for my ethnography instead of the enduring the long delay that would be involved if I first used my research as my doctoral dissertation. Also, in the spring of 1972, when I told Dave that I had to teach summer session to support my family and would not be able to devote all my summer to writing, he arranged for Holt to pay me an advance on royalties equal to what I would earn teaching summer session. By June, 1973, I had completed the manuscript and *Chicano Prisoners* was in print by June, 1974.

I believe it was in 1972 when Joe Gonzo, a tall, lanky, nearly 30 to 35-year-old student enrolled in one of my cultural anthropology classes. He had a distinctive name which I did not forget. He sat in the back row and frequently asked questions, particularly about Chicanos and my research. I can't recall the specific subtle things that made me suspicious, but I strongly suspected that he might be an undercover agent. He abruptly missed the first midterm exam and dropped the class—without a word being said to me.

In 1974 or '75, in one of my cultural anthropology classes, as I was taking the college-required roll, calling last names; each student was responding with his or her first name. This was the way I normally began the task of connecting my students' names with their faces. I was surprised and did a double take when I saw Joe Gonzo's name. I immediately looked at the back row, saw Joe and said "Joe! Joe Gonzo. You're back again."

Joe looked startled and asked, "You recognize me?" I assured him that I obviously did, that he started the same class with me a couple years earlier and that he had dropped out before the first midterm. He seemed to squirm as he said something about having had to leave for an emergency. My much earlier suspicion that he was an undercover agent seemed to be confirmed by his awkward reaction to my recognizing him. Hiding my private amusement at being able to give someone I now firmly believed was an undercover agent a bad time, I told him I hoped he would make it through the full semester this time. He never returned to class. I never saw him again.

In addition to spending hours writing my ethnography and teaching anthropology classes, I continued my involvement with Ed Aguirre and others in the Chicano movement. I was delighted when, after a couple of years, I was granted tenure at El Camino. Then, after I completed the manuscript for *Chicano Prisoners* and it was being prepared for publication in 1974, I decided to reveal the burden I had hidden from everyone at El Camino.

I met with Dr. Marsee, President of El Camino College. I revealed much of what had happened at Cabrillo College regarding my being "not rehired" and my suspicions about my phone being tapped by the FBI. I do recall specifically one of Dr. Marsee's comments. Near the end of our conversation he admitted that I must feel much better having revealed my secret and that the FBI was wrong to have done that. Then he said that, had there been a call to him from the FBI after I was interviewed for my position, he would not have let that influence their decision to hire me. Then he proudly added, "We're not that provincial here."

Hiding my feelings, I laughed inside to myself. I had strong feelings that *if* the FBI had made the same call to Marsee that they had made to other administrators at other colleges and universities at that time, Marsee would have capitulated and I would have received the "I'm sorry Mr. Davidson, but we've already hired someone for that position" phone call.

CHICANO PRISONERS IN PRINT

In 1974, with the publication of *Chicano Prisoners: The Key to San Quentin*, the pace of my activities dramatically increased. The reaction to my book was more than gratifying. Let me share a few examples of that praise.

Ralph Guzman, Assistant Director of the Mexican-American Study Project at UCLA, author of several books, and well known and highly respected in the Chicano community and by Chicano scholars, wrote a glowing letter of praise to me regarding my book.

I received similar letters of praise from anthropology professors Gerry Berreman at U.C. Berkeley and Dan Crowley at U.C. Davis. Comparable reaction came from other scholars—in written and verbal form. Some social and behavioral scientists commented on my engaging style, noting that they just couldn't put it down.

A Cal State University, Los Angeles instructor who taught a Chicano Psychology course was very enthusiastic about my book. Not only was he using it in his class, his wife (an ex-student of mine who directly knew of Family [Mexican Mafia] through her brother), claimed, "It's the bible around the house."

Laud Humphreys, the author of *Tearoom Trade* and *Out of the Closet*, was using my book in a course he was teaching on the Prison Experience at Pitzer College (one of the Claremont Colleges east of Los Angeles). He had so many positive things to say about my book that I cannot remember all of them. He said he was going to nominate my book for the C. Wright Mills Award. Later I gave a guest talk to one of his classes.

Marshall Lumsden, the editor of *Human Behavior*, the magazine of the Social Sciences, felt that the article "Family Secrets" by Susan Stocking, which appeared in the November, 1974 issue of his magazine would give my book considerable publicity. Susan had read my book and later interviewed me for her article. In her article she concluded, "Turn an anthropologist loose in a large prison to study subcultures, and he's likely to come up with some surprising information. More, in fact, than some people would like to have known." There were a few factual errors in the article; however, I thought they were far outweighed by the positive aspects.

Carey McWilliams, Editor of *The Nation*, commented in a review: "An excellent study of prison culture...Davidson tells it like it is...the materials and observations are fascinating."

The Royal Anthropological Institute of Great Britain and Ireland, in one of the "Comment" sections of its journal praised my book, noting, "It is a remarkable analysis of the dominance of the well-known North Californian prison by the Mexican mafia...."

I was asked to give guest talks at many universities and colleges—from UCLA, U.C. Riverside and USC; to California State Universities at Los Angeles, Long Beach and Dominguez Hills; and colleges such as Claremont and others. The classes I talked with included the subjects of cultural anthropology, applied anthropology, criminology, penology, Chicano studies and Chicano psychology.

In the greater Los Angeles area, for several years, I was guest speaker for many organizations, ranging from Rotary and Lions Clubs to the American Legion and MALDEF (Mexican-American Legal Defense Fund). Also—after all the negative things that had been directed at me by CDC—I was amazed when I was asked to give talks at the annual meeting of the Southern California Probation and Parole Association. What I had to say about the *real* prison system and Chicanos was so well-received that they asked me to participate at their next annual meeting.

Owing to the persisting ignorance of most California legislators about what actually was going on regarding prisons and CDC, I sent copies of my book, along with a personal letter, to several selected legislators in Sacramento.

I had wondered how I could express my gratitude to some of the convicts—those still in prison in 1974—who taught me so much about their subculture. For those still in prison, I was able to send them a copy of *Chicano Prisoners* so they could see the results of my promise to "tell it like it is." Let me explain. If I openly attempted to mail a book to a convict, it would have been caught by staff censors and destroyed. However, I knew that if a prisoner had money in his "inmate account," he could order and pay for an approved book through the prison library. Later, he would be able to receive the book in an unopened mailer from the publisher with the publisher's name and return address on the outside. The censors would not open the mailer unless from some unapproved publisher.

So, several times I contacted Holt and had them send a copy of my book to a particular convict, including his name and number. Soon the convict would receive a copy of my book, hidden inside Holt's inconspicuous, unopened mailer. I often wondered how the convicts reacted when they opened their unexpected gift.

For convicts who had been paroled or discharged to the streets, it was easy for me to personally thank them and give them a copy of my book. Soon, I was surprised when I discovered an unexpected, positive use of my book. An ex-convict told me that years earlier he had found it difficult to talk about prison with a close relative (the same applied to a close friend) who had never been in prison. The close relative usually was inclined to think the ex-convict was coming off-the-wall and grossly exaggerating when he would relate things about prison. Unfortunately, many times this precluded additional discussions about prison. However, after publication of my book, the ex-convict said he gave a copy of my book to his close relative to read. Then, after reading my book, the relative knew enough about life inside prison to be able to hold a reasonable conversation about prison with the ex-convict.

Recognizing the substantial market for my book outside of anthropology, Dave Boynton wrote to me in November, 1974, indicating that it was Holt's intention to advertise my book in journals that have to do with criminology, penology, Chicanos and prisons. Dave indicated that Holt was going to promote my book more broadly than they have done in the past for the 84 ethnographies in their extensive Case Studies in Cultural Anthropology series—which covers cultures and subcultures from around the world. In addition, my book also was going to be included in a separate series—Case Studies in Contemporary American Culture that was being promoted by Holt.

Within a few years, Carter, Glasser and Wilkins published the Second Edition of their college textbook titled *Correctional Institutions.* Included in their textbook was my entire, truly unique, detailed 46 page section, "The Prisoner Economy" from *Chicano Prisoners.*

In 1978, Holt published an anthology of case studies in cultural anthropology titled: *Urban Anthropology in the United States, Four Cases,* edited by George and Louise Spindler of Stanford University. The anthology included four case studies: *Chicano Prisoners* by Davidson, *Portland Longshoremen* by Pilcher, *Lifelines* by Aschenbrenner, and *Fun City* by Jacobs. Later, three of the four case studies were reissued in the Case Studies by Waveland Series.

Disturbing events

Wrongly Convicted

For years I continued my extremely close relationship with ML, my Chicano-convict friend who was one of the founding leaders of what came to be commonly called the *Mexican Mafia* and who was an editor of *The Outlaw*. After I was kicked out of San Quentin, ML remained inside for several years; we communicated via the US mail, but the depth and warmth of earlier conversations was lacking owing to probable censorship by guards. I missed some of the memorable events we shared.

For example, I still shake my head and smile when I recall one day when I was talking with ML as he was working at one of his prison jobs—tending some roses in the small garden on the south side of the prison hospital. Unexpectedly, Warden Nelson walked toward ML and me. As Big Red passed, ML glared at him, gave him the finger and angrily said, "Fuck you Red!" I was shocked by what ML had done and the potentially negative reaction that might occur from Big Red. However, the Warden merely glared straight ahead, said nothing and continued walking. I looked at ML and shook my head in disbelief. ML merely commented that what had taken place was nothing compared to other things in the past that were much more important. ML and Big Red knew each other well from years of conflict. I was amused at ML's temerity. ML knew how to predict and use even the warden.

Almost any other prisoner probably would have been thrown in the hole for doing what ML had done.

Even though ML had multiple sclerosis—with some early symptoms of impaired vision, and unsteadiness in walking and maintaining balance—it appeared that he would be in prison for many more years. For me, he was an excellent teacher who adeptly taught me so much about the prisoners' culture. With walls between us, I missed his insight into and knowledge of the depths of that culture.

After 1971, when I was living in Redondo Beach and teaching at El Camino College, I was surprised to get a phone call from ML. He had been let out on parole and was living in Costa Mesa with a relative. Some way, a psychiatrist had convinced the Adult Authority to parole ML. (Personally, I wondered if San Quentin administrators might have been behind ML's surprise release as a way to get rid of this thorn in their side.)

Bear in mind, by 1971, when ML was paroled, he had spent about half his adult life in prison. Understandably, when he was paroled on the streets, at times he had what appeared to be the social skills of an 18-year-old. This was significantly different from his exceptional cultural skills inside prison. Now, ML wanted to sow some oats—frequenting bars, dating gals, and driving sporty cars. Fortunately, ML's multiple sclerosis went into remission after he was paroled, so he was able to obtain a drivers license and legally drive.

ML and I soon expanded our close friendship to include my wife and two young children. He took great pleasure visiting and having meals with us, and becoming involved in many of our family activities. I'll never forget a couple of mental images of ML: Pulling a giant yellow and black bumble bee pull toy to the delight of my young daughter. Being the oldest and biggest *kid* at my young son's birthday party as he vainly tried, while blindfolded, to break the pinata with a long stick. My kids loved him, and the feeling was mutual.

One time ML took my family and me to Disneyland. With him, the five of us had a wonderful, memorable time. He insisted it was his treat. Later he told me that our day at Disneyland was not only great fun for him, it was a way he could begin to pay us back for all we had done for him. More than once he told my wife and me that we were the first real family he had—especially the kids that he never had.

Soon ML had a girlfriend (NG). She joined ML in many activities such as dinner at our home and with them at restaurants in Costa Mesa.

One day I received a phone call from ML. He was furious! He had purchased a used Ford Mustang from a used car salesman who told ML that if anything went wrong with it to bring it back and he would have it fixed for free. Accustomed to verbal agreements in prison and expecting someone to live up to his word, ML had nothing in writing—just the word of the salesman. A week or so after ML bought the car, something broke and immediately needed major repair. When ML called and asked to have the Mustang repaired free of charge, the salesman said "No!" He indicated that nothing was in writing, so ML would have to pay for any repairs. ML protested, noting what the salesman had verbally promised. The response still was "No!" ML insisted and threatened, but the salesman was not impressed and would not change his mind.

Fortunately ML called me, and explained the situation. ML was ready to inflict serious bodily harm or more on the salesman who would not live up to his word. I convinced ML to wait until I talked with the salesman. I immediately drove to Costa Mesa to talk some sense into the salesman. My explanation of some of ML's background—including ML's expectation from his years of experience in prison that a man's word is gold, and that the consequences for not living up to one's word could result in severe bodily harm or more—terrified the salesman! While I was there, he immediately called ML and told him to bring the Mustang in and the repairs would be done free of charge. The salesman lived up to his word.

Not too long later, ML traded his Mustang in on a very sharp-looking used white MGB. He dropped by to show my family and me his pride and joy. Being a two-seater, it took quite a while for him to give each of us an exciting ride. My wife was thrilled; ML even let her drive it a bit. She loved it and several times suggested that we should get one like it too.

In the Fall of 1972, in addition to teaching my courses at El Camino, I was in the midst of spending as much time as possible to complete my writing of *Chicano Prisoners*. One weekend my wife and kids went to visit one of my sisters. This was to give me a nice block of uninterrupted time to devote to writing. However, early *Saturday evening* the phone rang. ML wanted to come up and visit for the evening. At first, I was disappointed but did not mention to ML that my writing would be interrupted. Soon after he arrived, we went to a jazz club near the beach in Hermosa Beach. Later, at home, we had a couple more beers and talked. When ML had to leave, we realized that he had consumed too much beer to safely drive home so he could feed his animals. He decided they could wait until morning; so he slept on the couch Saturday night.

On *Sunday morning*, ML got in his white MGB, and I knelt down beside it as we continued our conversation. I don't recall the details of the conversation but I do remember how nice the warm fall sunshine felt on my back. Before ML left, Gale McCall, my next door neighbor—a retired bookkeeper—came out to get his Sunday paper from his driveway. He came over to look at ML's sporty little car, exchange greetings and briefly talk. I introduced him to ML. Soon Gale left and ML drove off to feed his animals in Costa Mesa.

Within about a week, I was shocked by a phone call from NG. *ML had been arrested for the murder of a woman!* Apparently ML was the last person to have been seen with the murdered woman—having a couple of drinks with her in a Costa Mesa bar on *Friday evening—the day before he spent the Saturday evening and night with me in Redondo Beach!* The police had discovered the murdered woman's body—apparently dumped near a road in the Chino Hills area—mid-morning on *Sunday*. The authorities were not able to say exactly when the woman was murdered, but they were able to determine that her body was dumped there between about 2:00 a.m. and 9:30 a.m. on *Sunday morning!* ML readily admitted that he had a couple of drinks with the woman on that *Friday* evening, but that was all. He did *not* see her on Saturday or Sunday. The press soon reported this as the "Chino Hills Murder."

Within days, two detectives from the San Bernardino County Sheriff Department came to my home and extensively questioned me, recording our conversation. I detailed what had happened on the critical

Saturday night and Sunday morning, also noting that Gale McCall had talked with ML and me on that Sunday morning when the woman's body was dumped off a road near Chino.

The authorities kept ML locked up, regardless of what I had shared with them. So I visited ML in the San Bernardino County Jail to try to find out from ML why he was not being released. I don't recall many of the details of my conversation with ML—both of us still were incredulous and shocked.

The "Chino Hills Murder" case went to trial. I was to testify in ML's defense—as was Gale McCall. I gave testimony, responding to the Defense Attorney's questions which enabled me to tell what had occurred on the critical Saturday evening and Sunday morning.

Then the District Attorney took over. He repeatedly tried to trip me up and get me to say something that would incriminate ML—and probably me for perjury. ML's attorney had thought my testimony would quickly be over; but the DA—being able to bring up my research in San Quentin and past friendship with ML—tenaciously persisted. I do not recall the specifics of the DA's interrogation of me because I was so intensely busy double-thinking every question and my answer—which immediately was followed by another question—that I had no time to remember the preceding question and answer. I do recall that during most of this interrogation, the questions about my research and long-term friendship with ML had little to do with the actual events of the critical Saturday evening and Sunday morning—events that were cut and dry for me, Gale McCall and ML. After about forty-five minutes, the judge recessed for lunch.

As ML's Defense attorney and I walked to lunch, we were joined by the DA. The two of them talked with each other, ignoring me, but not talking about ML's trial. From their conversation, I assumed they knew each other well. Suddenly their conversation briefly turned to something that shocked me. The DA jokingly told the Defense attorney, "Since I've only won two of the last five murder trials, it's my turn to win this one." The Defense attorney merely laughed. The two attorneys continued their rather lighthearted conversation through lunch and on the way back to court.

Having returned to the courtroom before the judge and others had returned, I walked up and stood near the defense table. The DA—

having already grilled me for 45 minutes before lunch—walked up and stood beside me. Then he asked me, "What do you know about the Mexican Mafia?"

I glared at him and coldly replied, "If you have any more questions for me, ask them when I'm on the witness stand." The DA merely turned and walked away. My mind raced—trying to figure out how I would respond if he asked a question about the Mexican Mafia while I was under oath, on the witness stand. To this day, I have never been sure what I would have done.

After the lunch recess, the DA grilled me for another forty-five minutes. I was relieved that he never asked me about the Mexican Mafia while I was on the witness stand.

Since I was not allowed to observe any of the other proceedings, I left the courtroom. In the hallway, I saw Gale McCall who was dressed in a dark blue suit, wearing an America Flag lapel pin. He was waiting to be escorted into the courtroom to give his testimony. I was exhausted from giving testimony for about one and half hours; but I felt that I had won all the skirmishes with the DA. I had done nothing to discredit myself or my testimony.

I had taken a sick day from my teaching obligations at El Camino College (with the Dean's permission). However, I was unable to take additional time off to merely be an observer. And, I'm not sure that I would have been allowed by the court to do so.

A few days later I was shocked to hear that ML had been convicted!

I was ignorant of what transpired at the trial—other than what I endured the day I gave testimony. What had swayed the jury to convict ML? Had my testimony been ignored or discounted for some reason? There had been so many questions; but—regardless of my efforts—I was never able to learn additional details about what influenced the jury to bring about the injustice. It was, and still continues to be, a bitter pill for me to swallow—knowing that ML was innocent but unfairly convicted. I still become angry when I think of what happened.

ML ended up being sentenced and sent to Folsom Prison. Most likely, he would spend the rest of his life in prison. Henceforth, our communication would be limited to letters. ML no longer had any use for his sporty little MGB, so he gave it to my wife as a huge thank you gift. She was overwhelmed by the gift. It was interesting when we received the legal paperwork transferring the vehicle to my wife—a Mexican Mafia friend of mine whom I knew quite well in San Quentin (who had been transferred to Folsom Prison) signed the vehicle transfer papers as a witness to ML's signature. My wife truly appreciated and enjoyed her gift.

A few years later I learned that ML was dead. The *official* word from administrators at Folsom Prison was that ML had committed suicide in his cell—by hanging himself! I found that difficult to believe. I truly believe that he was killed by someone from one of the opposing major factions in the brutal conflict between the opposing groups of the Mexican Mafia.

ML's mother who lived in Costa Mesa had a memorial service for ML. I talked with the Dean of my Division at El Camino to take the day off to attend the service, but she refused. I argued that ML *truly was like a brother to me*, but she still refused. The following day I went anyway, being absent from my classes. The Dean was furious. She docked my next paycheck. I was disappointed by the Dean's actions. I should have merely not said anything to her in the first place and called in sick to use one of my many accumulated sick days.

DEATH THREAT

Soon after the publication of *Chicano Prisoners* in 1974, I decided to write a book depicting the *life history* of SB a Chicano prisoner-parolee-friend. I had intended to use his life as an example of what it is like to be born and raised in the barrio and later to move into street gangs and then prison gangs. The *life history* book was first to be used as my doctoral dissertation at U.C. Davis. Then—after slight changes—the book was to be published by Holt, Rinehart and Winston.

I met SB at his prisoner job in San Quentin soon after I began my research. We immediately hit it off well and soon were having long conversations. After a short time we became close friends. After I was kicked out of San Quentin by the staff in 1968, and after SB was later paroled, we renewed our friendship, which immediately included our wives and children. Reciprocal family visits were frequent and enjoyable, both in his home and mine.

After receiving the go-ahead from Holt regarding their publishing of my to- be-delayed *life history* book, I discussed the book with SB—it would be about *his* life. We both were excited about collaborating on the book. This would entail my using a tape recorder for the first time in my research in order to preserve our conversations. We met many times and soon became accustomed to the tape recorder—something I had never used before—particularly in San Quentin. SB and I were delighted with the amount of material we were generating on tape.

On the evening of February 13, 1976, I received a shockingly unbelievable, rather frantic phone call from SB! I surmised from his excited exclamations that something was wrong with him physically, or that something potentially deadly had occurred. Before I could even ask what specifically was wrong with him, he forcefully demanded, "Are you going to write the book about me?" I was taken-aback. He knew I was going to write the book *after* I gathered enough material. His tone of voice seemed to reinforce my assumption that something—possibly even deadly—had happened.

I started to explain that I didn't have nearly enough material on tape yet to even begin the actual organization and writing of the book. SB angrily interrupted, "If you *aren't* going to write the book, then I'm going to make a phone call and *you'll be dead—and your wife and kids too!* I know where your wife works and your kids go to school—*all of you'll be dead!*"

I was shocked, dumbfounded! From his tone of voice I seemed certain that his threat was real. As I tried to conceive of a way to respond without actually saying that I would *not* write the book, SB interrupted, "If you *are* going to write the book, tell me; that'll be fine. I'll make a call, and *they'll make sure that you do write it! If you say you will, but then don't write it in the future, all of you will end up dead!*"

I felt that I couldn't say *yes*, or *no*! He kept asking if I *was* or *was not* going to write the book! I kept hedging, not saying yes or no. Finally— thinking he was soon going to die, I told him that I'd do what I could for his wife and his kids. My hedging without saying yes or no, and my offer to help his family, coupled with his insistence that I say yes or no probably lasted about five minutes—but is seemed like twenty.

Abruptly SB was pulled away from the phone. A male voice told me SB was being taken to the hospital by the paramedics and then hung up.

The death threat had been made! I had not answered yes or no! What had happened to SB? I assumed the death threat had not miraculously disappeared.

I made several rather frantic phone calls, trying to find out what had happened and what might still happen. Finally I discovered that SB had been in a knock-down drag-out fight with his wife. SB was a large, formidable man; his wife was just as tall and was an even match in a fight. They had broken every breakable thing in their house. It was the sheriff who arrested SB and had him taken to the hospital.

What about SB's health? I learned that he had slipped and severely cut his butt on a broken bottle! It took 47 stitches to sew him up! I was unable to contact SB. He had been taken from the hospital and tightly locked up in jail.

My mind was racing. I speculated as to why SB had suddenly, irrationally turned against me. Was he high on something or drunk? Was it possible that he thought he was going to bleed to death and his menacing call to me had been an attempt to get some financial insurance for his wife and kids in the future. (He apparently was ignorant of how little actually is earned from a book.)

One of my phone contacts indicated that—since SB had not yet rescinded the death threat—the threat still existed! My contact and I knew that SB had the means to have the threat carried out. It would be impossible for me or any of my contacts to talk with SB while he was in jail.

After a sleepless night, the next morning, following my typical routine, I went to the college to teach my Friday classes. But, before classes began I realized I couldn't do that. I had a colleague cover for me with some excuse, called home, picked up my wife and two kids and drove to my in-laws who lived in Palm Desert.

My father-in-law was very close to dying of leukemia. We had planned perhaps our last visit to be on Saturday. Instead, we arrived Friday, a day early. He died that evening while we were there. My mother-in-law repeatedly said it was an "act of God that we were there." She was ignorant of *why* we were a day early. Also, she was unaware of the nature of the many phone calls I made that Friday.

Within a couple of days, three people contacted me. One was someone I knew—I trusted him. But, I did not know the other two; however, both claimed they knew who I was and what I had done on behalf of Chicanos and prisoners; they felt that no one should threaten me with death. Each of the three had independently contacted me, each at a different time. And, each of the three indicated that he would get rid of my problem for me! Not wanting any of them to kill SB, I declined each offer, stating that I would take care of it my own way. At that time, I had no idea how or when I would get out from under the threat.

Regarding the two I did not know, who offered to get rid of my problem, I wondered who they might actually be—from *La EME* or *Nuestra Familia*? Or, were they the result of the possible tapping of my phone by the FBI or some other agency; if so, they could have been undercover agent provocateurs attempting to set me up for ordering an execution.

My family and I stayed away from our home until Sunday when my father-in-law's funeral was to take place. Unfortunately, there was something that we needed from our home in Redondo Beach—we had arrived Friday in casual clothes, but needed clothes appropriate for the funeral. Cautiously, fearful of the death threat, I did several things: made a short list of only the clothes that we would wear to the funeral; called a neighbor to confirm that no one was parked watching our place; rapidly drove past our home several times; suddenly stopped in front of the house, dashed inside, grabbed the clothes, and rushed outside. Then I raced away to the funeral.

Soon SB was released from jail and was at home. His wife answered the phone and indicated that SB was sound asleep and heavily medicated because of the pain. Without revealing *why* I was calling (not knowing if she knew of the death threat) I merely told her that I'd call SB later. I was frustrated. I had thought that I could rationally talk with SB, get him to understand my position and rescind the threat.

Searching for another way to eliminate the threat, I was advised by a leader of the Chicano movement in Texas to contact a particular individual—called NJ. He had an office in Inglewood and was actively involved in the Chicano movement in the Los Angeles area, dealing with several governmental agencies. In discussing the situation and how to proceed, NJ and I recognized that SB might be reluctant to admit that he had made an irrational error, that he might feel such an admission or apology would be a challenge to his *machismo*—it would *not* be *macho* to back down.

It took considerable time for NJ and me to make arrangements behind the scenes. During that time, SB had recovered enough to be seen back on the streets, but he had not approached me to apologize or to cancel the death threat. It continued to be a frightening time for me and my family.

Finally, six very long, stressful weeks after the threat was made— with NJ acting as the older, mature mediator on behalf of one of the influential leaders of the Chicano movement in Texas—SB met with NJ and me at NJ's office. We were tense but civil as we carried out our agreed-upon plan. One by one I played the start of a cassette long enough for SB to recognize what it was. Then I would eject and cut the cassette in half with some shears. This was repeated until all of my cassettes had been destroyed. Little was said, but before we parted we gave each other an *abrazo* (a hug); and for SB and me, it meant that if we met again on the streets, we could be at least be perfunctorily pleasant.

I never did learn why he put me and my family under a death threat. However, without resorting to the three offers made to me to get rid of my problem, bloodshed was avoided and SB and I have been able to go on our own ways. I never saw SB again.

Since my efforts to write a *life history* about SB had abruptly ended, I had to reconsider what I would do regarding obtaining my PhD at U.C. Davis. I had earlier taken a leave of absence to compile information and write my doctoral dissertation about SB. That was to be followed by a slightly different version of the same material which would be the subject of my next book which Holt wanted to publish. I had not considered doing a *life history* of any one other than SB and no other Chicano immediately came to mind.

Something quite unexpected soon occurred. Since my prospects at UC Davis did not look too promising, I shared my concerns with NJ. He came up with an alternative. He claimed he had been in close contact with officials at the University of Washington. He was going to become their Director of Chicano studies starting the fall semester, 1976. He offered me a teaching position in that department. I questioned this because I was not a Chicano. He laughed and noted that I could be the token Anglo in the Chicano studies program—one that knew as much or more about the Chicano culture than many less-educated Chicanos do. I would be a welcome asset. Then he revealed—in addition—he would be able to guarantee that my activities would lead to my obtaining a PhD from the University of Washington. It was an interesting offer which I seriously considered.

I would have to permanently cut my ties with U.C. Davis. I would have to sell or rent our home in Redondo Beach. I would have to find a place to live near the University of Washington. Then I would have to give El Camino College notice that I would not return for the fall semester. Time was short. I needed something in writing from NJ and the University of Washington. More time passed, so I finally called the University of Washington; *they had never heard of NJ!*

I was shocked. Was NJ an undercover agent? Was this the FBI's latest attempt to destroy my ability to make a living as an anthropologist? This appeared to be not unlike the unsuccessful attempts to devastate me and my family when they fired me from Cabrillo College.

I contacted the leader of the Chicano movement in Texas who had advised me to contact NJ. The leader was extremely apologetic. He had just discovered through another source that NJ was a scam artist! The leader personally believed that NJ possibly was not an FBI agent, but just a con artist who had been able to bluff his way into the position he held and get paid for holding that position. I disagreed, arguing that in retrospect I had missed some red warning flags.

I was furious that I had been duped by NJ. I immediately cut my ties with him and thought I'd never look back. However, when I *did* look back, I realized that he did accomplish one positive thing. He successfully extracted me from SB's death threat without anyone resorting to violence.

Soon, SJ, a Chicano friend who was teaching at California State University San Jose, contacted me regarding the University's expanding Chicano Studies Program. He suggested that I apply for one of the new positions. He felt I was better-qualified than the other applicants for the position. My resume and application proved SJ was correct—I was better qualified. However, there was a serious problem that members of the selection committee would not ignore—I was not Chicano and my name was wrong. SJ told me that it was a blatant example of reverse discrimination and that I should fight the committee's decision. I refused to do so. I assured SJ that I understood why the committee chose someone who was less-qualified—he was born and raised in a barrio and his name definitely was a Chicano one. His name and background was more important to the committee.

For some time, I put my research activities on the back burner. I kept in touch with many Chicano friends, but I did little active participation. I still gave guest talks and lectures, but I became more and more disillusioned that anything was actually going to bring about legitimate legislative changes that would be necessary to correct the relatively secret abuses of prisoners by staff throughout CDC.

In 1978 I started toying with several ideas: of completely backing off from my diminishing research interests; of cutting almost all of my ties with my earlier Chicano contacts; and of abandoning my efforts to pursue a PhD in anthropology.

In December, 1978, a member of the Mexican Mafia informed me about something that had just taken place at a beautiful, isolated

Mexican Mafia rancheria in Baja California where my wife and I had recently been invited to visit as guests. There had been a particularly violent encounter between the Mexican Mafia and *Los Federales* (the Mexican Federal Police). The *Federales* raided the rancheria. The ensuing shootout resulted in several *Federales* being killed and the Mexican Mafia members abandoning their rancheria. Suddenly it was deserted.

This incident had a chilling effect on me. For some time I had been aware that the conflict between the opposing major factions of the Mexican Mafia had become more violent. I had no desire to continue with my contacts and risk the danger of being involved—danger for both myself and my family. Also, I realized that I was well-established as an anthropology professor and had published *Chicano Prisoners: The Key to San Quentin* in **THE** most prestigious series in anthropology at that time. Consequently, *I made the major decision to not pursue my efforts for a PhD. I cut my San Quentin and Chicano ties. Regarding the Mexican Mafia, I would write or say <u>nothing more</u> than what I wrote about in 1972 and was published in* **Chicano Prisoners** *in 1974.*

New Direction

While I was on Christmas-New Year vacation from El Camino College, I checked my phone messages at the college. There were several messages from someone who wanted me to call him. Since I didn't know who he was, I decided to wait until I returned from vacation to return his calls. So, in January, 1979, I called him.

Everett Freeman was one of the old time writer-producers in Hollywood who had an impressive list of credits. He indicated that he was writing a screenplay that would be largely set inside prison. He had read everything he could about prisons and felt that my book (*Chicano Prisoners*) was the most balanced treatment, so he wanted to talk with me.

We met for lunch at a restaurant and talked for about three hours. Finally he told me that—since he was getting so much more from our conversation than he had anticipated—he would share credit on the script with me. I truly did not realize what that would be.

For a few months we either met at his home in Westwood or talked over the phone, almost every day. It was quite exciting for me. I was amused that several times I had to tell Ev that he couldn't include something in the screenplay. He frequently wanted to add some tough-guy, James Cagney bits, and I told him we couldn't—it would be unrealistic. Also, during the spring, I audited a screenwriting seminar that Ev was teaching at UCLA.

Near the end of spring, we had completed the first draft of our screenplay. Then, unfortunately, Ev had a stroke! After he recovered, we had a long conversation. He suggested that I turn my writing talents to screenwriting. I took his advice.

It was interesting to me that my research in San Quentin and my book had quite unexpectedly turned my life in a new direction.

The first screenplay I wrote was a learning experience that I never showed to anyone. It did not live up to my own expectations. I continued writing screenplays, and I also taught screenwriting workshops at El Camino until I took early retirement in December, 1993.

Six other screenplays followed between 1980 and 1985: *Gold Creek, One Less Bull, Grannie Annie, Escape From Law, Feud, Fish Bull*; and *Suddenly Silent* was written in 2005.

Fish Bull (meaning "New Guard" to the prisoners) is about a mid-level, unemployed executive who, in financial desperation, takes a job as a guard at San Quentin Prison and is shocked and morally revulsed by the brutal reality behind the walls as he is tricked and pressured into illegal acts he never imagined he could commit! It is quite realistic.

Unfortunately, I personally did *not* have great connections in Hollywood such as a relative or an influential friend. Often I was asked by an agent if I had screenwriting credits. When I said no, it seemed that the stock answer was, "Well, come back when you do."

The last agent I did have—for *Feud* and *Fish Bull*—finally, after having me dangling on a hook for 13 months, apologized and said, "Ted, I'm sorry, but I have several writers who do have credits. It's so much easier to place their screenplays than for someone without credits. I have to devote my efforts to them." I did not tell him what I really thought about him at that time.

Disgusted with agents, I decided to turn myself into an expert on the Donner Party and write a *screenplay* that would vividly bring the shocking details of one of the most riveting tragedies of American history to life.

To become an expert on the Donner Party, I read reams of books, dug through original documents at the Bancroft Historical Library, 4-wheeled out the Donner trail from the Continental Divide two times, hiked and 4-wheeled the trail over the Sierra many times, snowshoed across Donner Pass atop snow more than twenty feet deep, and vicariously lived and re-lived the experiences of the principal characters in order to empathize with them and accurately bring them back to life.

I did not focus on George Donner, who was *not* the real leader of the party and never reached the lake, peak and pass named for him. Instead, I focused on Jim Reed (*the real leader*), Maggie Reed (Jim's wife) and Bill Eddy (the best hunter in the party). By focusing on these three, I am able to breathe life into all the historically accurate, astonishing events faced by the party—extraordinary confrontations with life and death; courage and cowardice; starvation, madness and murder; love and hate; cannibalism and survival.

Three times I gave away free options for my eight-hour miniseries screenplay. Each time it took 18 months for the person I dealt with to conclude that it was "just too big" for him to handle.

Frustrated, I finally decided to turn the screenplay into an historical novel, using all the same material but presenting it in a different format. My efforts with literary agents resulted in comments that "historical novels are difficult to place, and there's not much money to be made on them."

Finally, I was able to publish *Donner-Reed Tragedy* through Writers Club Press in 2002. I was extremely pleased that my book was highly regarded by Donner Party experts and reviewers. Since publication of the book, my efforts to have the screenplay version of *Donner-Reed Tragedy* produced have yet to succeed. I personally feel that the miniseries could find a receptive audience on PBS.

As an aside, for those who might be interested in my book and screenplay, I do have a website that contains a considerable amount about my Donner works on it. www.donner-reed.com

Thus, in a round about way, I was unexpectedly drawn in this new direction by my earlier research among Chicanos at San Quentin. With the writing of my earlier screenplays; the research and writing of *Donner-Reed Tragedy* as a screenplay and novel, and my writing of *Suddenly Silent*, my latest screenplay before this memoir, I continue to actively write.

My considered refusals

American Me, the movie

In 1990, I was pulled back into involvement with Chicanos and prisoners. I received a call from a woman who was involved in the production of *American Me*, a yet-to-be-produced film to be directed by Edward James Olmos—he also was to star as the movie's main character. The film was to treat the life of Santana (Edward James Olmos), a young Los Angeles Chicano who breaks the law and ultimately ends up in Folsom Prison as the leader of a powerful gang—both inside and outside of prison. The film was to introduce viewers to some of the reality of gang life—both on the streets and inside prison.

The film sounded quite interesting to me for two reasons. **First**, since I had earlier, in 1976, started to write a book depicting the life history of a Chicano prisoner-parolee-friend, using his life as an example of what it is like to be born and raised in the barrio and subsequently to move into street gangs and then prison gangs. Unfortunately my writing of that book abruptly ceased in 1976 when I was quite unexpectedly put under an unmerited death threat (which I treated earlier in this work). **Second**, much later, in 1985, I had written *Fish Bull*, a screenplay which was primarily set inside Quentin Prison.

Initially I thought that *American Me* had considerable potential. The woman wanted me to become a technical advisor and possibly do some of the writing of the script. However, beyond my immediate interest and assessment of her offer, I soon became reluctant to become involved as an advisor or writer. I knew—from writing screenplays and teaching screenwriting workshops—that *a writer or technical advisor usually has little or no control over the end product that is released to the public as a movie.* The proposed subject of the Olmos movie did have considerable potential, but it also contained possibly dangerous or even deadly results for those involved in making the film. So, I refused the woman's request.

I attended the first showing of *American Me* when it was released in *1992*. I was one of probably ten Anglos at the most in the theater which was nearly filled with Chicanos. When the film was over and the audience exited the theater, every person that I could see appeared to have been seriously impressed by the film—some looked quite grim or even angry. There was little if any conversation.

American Me was generally viewed favorably by film critics in March, 1992. For example, *Chicago Sun-Times'* reviewer Roger Ebert liked the film and wrote that it "rang true" and appeared to be based on true situations. I had mixed feelings about Ebert's comments. Instinctively I felt that members of the Mexican Mafia might be offended by some parts of the film. In particular, there was one strikingly unrealistic, **non**-*macho* scene that probably would prove *extremely* infuriating. That scene depicted an excessively brutal, fictional homosexual rape in prison which violated the Mexican Mafia's sense of *machismo.*

My instinctive initial reaction apparently was correct. During the Los Angeles trial involving 12 Mexican Mafia members, news reports in 1996 and 1997 indicated that a leader of the Mexican Mafia *was* offended by *American Me*—particularly the fictional (non-*macho*) brutal rape in the film of one of the gang's founders. Consequently, the Mexican Mafia attempted to extort money from Olmos. Additionally it was reported that three technical advisors on the film were murdered by the Mexican Mafia—one being Ana Lizarraga, an East Los Angeles gang counselor.

MEXICAN MAFIA TRIAL, 1996-97

In his October 25, 1996 letter to me, Isaac Guillen, a third year Law Clerk, with the Federal Public Defenders Office in Los Angeles, indicated, "I am working on a case that involves a Latino prison gang. I read your book *Chicano Prisoners: The Key to San Quentin,* and am convinced that you could be of great help. I would like to speak with you regarding the possibility of hiring you as either an expert in 'Latino Prison Culture' or as an advisor in that area." His letter continued, "I understand that your book was written a while back, but the 'Chicano-Black Continuum' that you speak of exists today and is part of our case. I would greatly appreciate any assistance that you could provide...."

In the first of several phone conversations that followed, I indicated that I would need more information about what was involved. Mr. Guillen explained that he was working for the defense on a case that involved 21 members of the Mexican Mafia—13 of those were defendants. He indicated that in April, 1995 the defendants were arrested and charged with conspiring under the federal Racketeer Influenced and Corrupt Organization Act (RICO) and with murder.

Immediately I was guarded, prudently hiding my strong suspicion! To satisfy my personal curiosity, I *did* want to find out some details about the trial that was scheduled to begin in November, 1996, but *never* did I seriously even consider becoming an advisor or testifying. I knew getting involved, either as a witness or as an advisor could lead to fatal results.

Several phone conversations soon took place—one being a conference call involving Lindsey Weston, a defense attorney for one of the defendants in the case—her defendant had soon pleaded guilty. Guillen and Weston made several suggestions of things I should think about such as ideas that would suggest the Mexican Mafia does *not* have a cohesive enterprise on the streets and the paucity of *police* information, including how and where the police get it. A couple of their suggestions entailed things that I *absolutely could and would not do!* I saw too many *red flags*!

In response to my questioning, Guillen and Weston said that if I became an advisor, any application in writing by me to assist them would be "under seal." As to my questions about giving testimony in person at the trial, they didn't really respond except to note that the prosecution *could* interrogate me at length if they wanted to—another huge red flag!

Guillen and Weston revealed many other random things in the conference call, such as: There are 1,300 tapes of phone calls. Conversations and visiting room phones at Pelican Bay State Prison (the remote, super-secure prison in the northwest corner of California) were secretly taped. Two defendants would be brought in for the trial from Pelican Bay. Owing to many defense attorneys being involved on the case, numerous bad rulings already had been made. Also, *three advisors to the movie* American Me *by Edward James Olmos had been killed!*

Apparently trying to entice me with financial reward, Mr. Guillen pointed out that there already was up to $3,000 approved for advising, and more if needed. He indicated the fees for advising—$75 per hour (including being paid for phone conversations). For giving testimony on the witness stand as an expert it would be $150 per hour and possibly more. I was not tempted by the financial offers.

Of particular note to me were a few details revealed in one of the phone conversations about Mr. Castro, a snitch who appeared to be a prime informant who was helping prosecutors make a case against the Mexican Mafia that fit into RICO. The snitch *had been* an EME member, in his mid-thirties, facing life for manslaughter. For his cooperation with prosecutors, he had been put into the Federal Witness Protection program.

Being satisfied with some of the highlights of what the trial would involve and not wanting to waste any more of my time or Mr. Guillen's, I respectfully declined to become involved in the trial in any way. I realized that later I would probably learn a great deal more about the case—which would most likely be reported in the *Los Angles Times* at the conclusion of the trial.

On May 31, 1997, the *Los Angeles Times* published a detailed article headlined: "**12 Mexican Mafia Members Guilty in Racketeering Case.**" The article began: "In a major victory for federal prosecutors, 12 members of the Mexican Mafia were convicted Friday of racketeering and conspiracy charges, including murder and extortion carried out in a ruthless bid to extend the group's influence beyond California's prisons."

A few selected quotes from the lengthy article highlight some of the key points of the trial:

—"Federal authorities financed an 18-month investigation and collected more than 300 secret videotapes and audio recordings."

—"In all, 12 defendants were convicted of violating RICO and conspiracy to violate RICO. Most were found guilty of murdering seven people, including three advisors on Edward James Olmos' movie about the Mexican Mafia, 'American Me.'"

— "'The verdicts don't surprise me because I know of no other deadly group like the Eme,' said former Mexican Mafia member Ramon 'Mundo' Mendoza, who keeps his whereabouts a secret to avoid Eme reprisals. 'They are capable of killing people without a second's thought about it.'"

—"While the government scored the court victory over the Eme, the actual effect of the convictions on the streets is questionable, according to law enforcement experts who monitor the prison gang."

—"In recent months, while the case against the 13 defendants dragged on...Eme leaders have continued to meet with local street gangs, 'tax' their profits from drug sales and issue orders to carry out Mexican Mafia wishes...."

—"'I don't think the mob's going to shut down because of this,' said a veteran state corrections official, who asked not to be identified. 'They've come too far, and it's been too many years. I think it's [still] going to be business as usual.'"

—"One investigator called the verdict 'a double-edged sword.' Even though some of Eme's major leaders, who ruthlessly controlled street gangs, were convicted, a greater potential of violence exists because gang members may not be reined in as tightly when these leaders are dispersed across the federal prison system."

—"Among the 29 counts, the defendants were accused of killing seven people, most of them Eme members who fell out of favor. They also were accused of trying to kill 18 others, most of them gang members who refused to pay 'taxes' to the Eme."

—"Prosecutors held two trump cards—their star witness, Ernest 'Chuco' Castro and more than 300 videotapes and audio recordings that gave a rare look at how the prison gang operates. FBI agents were able to secretly record the tapes—in hotel rooms, parks and restaurants and over the telephone—with Castro's help."

—"Castro, 39, an admitted Mexican Mafia member and an ex-convict, agreed to cooperate with authorities after he was arrested in November 1993...."

—"Under the questioning of...the lead prosecutor in the case, Castro spent eight days describing the Eme and its inner workings, its rules about membership, its plans to tax street gangs, and the murder plots that were hatched at videotaped hotel meetings."

—"On cross-examination, Castro underwent weeks of intense grilling as defense attorneys accused him of being a murderous instigator who became a government informant to save his own skin after the weapons arrest. Without the government's help, he faced a lengthy prison term."

In the Postscript of *Chicano Prisoners: The Key to San Quentin*, I noted that the unity of Family no longer existed. Changes in 1972 had led to an extremely brutal power struggle between two major factions of Family in 1973. The bloodshed and deaths in the prisoner culture continued throughout CDC, and on the streets. That dynamic, rapidly-changing, power struggle was *not* something that I wanted to pursue at that time—it was well beyond the scope of what I was trying to do in my ethnography. Now, *More than thirty years since the publication of my book*, the power struggle still exists and has intensified.

In the December 1973 letter to George and Louise Spindler at Stanford University, General Editors of Holt's "Case Studies In Cultural Anthropology" Series, I wrote: "I deem it fortunate that I was given permission to 'carefully' portray *Family* in my book. To go beyond my postscript and detail further particulars about the Mafia-Familia warfare would be stepping beyond a 'careful' use of what I know. Such details would not only jeopardize certain individuals, they would also subject me to the prisoner sanctions that I have described in my book. In other words, not only will I refuse to betray the confidence given me, I will not do something that would possibly bring about my untimely death."

Now, more than thirty years later, the above quoted passage *still* is relevant. However, *now* I openly admit to being ignorant of any details regarding the over thirty years that the brutal power struggle has continued.

In closing, I do sincerely regret that legitimate legislative changes in the far-from-ideal California prison system have not occurred. Abuses of the ideal prison system by some staff members and administrators still occur behind those walls and probably will continue to do so far into the future. It is doubtful that the California legislature will soon be able to accomplish those necessary changes.

Also, quite unfortunately, I believe that—in spite of the efforts of Federal Authorities to end the power of the Mexican Mafia or destroy it—the Mexican Mafia will continue to thrive and grow.

In screenplays, it usually is best if there is a favorable ending. Unfortunately, I'm not able to provide that for my readers.

Conclusion

I openly admit that I am subject to the values that are an inherent part of being an anthropologist. In the past, when studying remote cultures—whether the peaceful bushmen of the Kalahari Desert or the often-deadly warriors of the Grand Valley in New Guinea—*the **goal** of the anthropologist was to learn that culture from the native's or informant's perspective, through the eyes of natives or informants, without judging or condemning.*

As the world grew smaller over many decades, most remote or isolated cultures have rapidly disappeared. Now we have a vast conglomeration of cultures and subcultures around the world, within single nations, and often within single cities.

Consequently—*with the same **goal** as noted above*—particularly since the late 1960's, anthropologists have turned to studying subcultures in larger national cultures. In the US, those studies have focused on subcultures such as the Amish, the Eskimo of North Alaska, Modern Blackfoot, Mexican-Americans of South Texas, a Hippie Ghetto, Portland Longshoremen, and Chicano Prisoners in San Quentin. All of these subcultures and *many more* are part of the larger, multicultural US culture. These subcultural studies by anthropologists have added to our depth of understanding of the complexities of the larger US culture.

I have felt pleased to be able to study a subculture in the United Sates that had never been the subject of anthropological research. Unfortunately, after I was kicked out of San Quentin and began openly sharing the results of my research with the public and particularly California state legislators—and later with the publication of my truly unique research in *Chicano Prisoners*—the extremely negative reaction of prison authorities was incredible. I seriously doubt that any anthropologist in the future will be given permission to do the kind of research I did in any prison.

The results of my holistic, secret-revealing research proved quite embarrassing for prison administrators and CDC officials. They repeatedly tried—often in illegal or immoral ways—to destroy my credibility, my professional life and my family. Obviously, I was not pleased with what was done to me by prison administrators, the FBI and possibly other governmental agencies or individuals. Frequently I was shocked, angered and saddened by their reprehensible and often illegal actions!

At times I have felt that *some* of those who run California prisons and CDC have tried to convince themselves—or hide from the public—that what they have abusively or illegally done to prisoners and others over the past decades is tolerable. In other words, it's acceptable to be monsters because they are fighting monsters.

For many years, prisoners who have protested against abuses of the prison system have publicly been called "militants" or "revolutionaries" by prison administrators. However, those protesting prisoners have usually been reasonable men who have endured years of abuse and who have finally protested against those abuses of the ideal prison system. They have been attempting to bring about legitimate changes which would bring the prison system back into accord with its ideals. The bitterness and frustration leading to these demonstrations have not been understood by the public. The prisoners' desperate, legitimate protests were the result of feelings that all legal means had failed them. The prisoners were willing to serve additional time in prison if they could bring the abuses to the public's attention.

Some of the protests have resulted in efforts by attorneys and state legislators to bring about changes in the prison system. However, those changes are few and have fallen short of what is needed. Unfortunately, usually the *real* causes of such protests have remained hidden from the public.

I regret that *Chicano Prisoners* no longer is in print, because there are *many extremely relevant things* about social control described in the book that still exist and continue to be insightful. Even though some things in San Quentin have changed considerably—such as in the "Postscript" where the forthcoming changes in the Mexican Mafia are only suggested—much in *Chicano Prisoners* still is useful for those who would want to understand what life can be like inside a huge prison.

As anthropologists often do, I studied a subculture where the behavior of subcultural members was dramatically different from my own subcultural behavior. I wanted to acquire the insider's perspective. So, *the prisoners became teachers*, who explained the different aspects of their culture. *They taught me how to see their world as they see it.* I observed, listened and asked questions. My convict teachers were glad to help. As my teachers—they taught me how to see and understand the prisoner subculture inside the prison and beyond.

In San Quentin, if I had been a prisoner, I would have entered as a "fish" or newcomer. A fish usually has to learn the prisoner culture the hard way unless he has help from other prisoners. Without some kind of help, it would take a fish many months or even a year or more to know the prisoner subculture well enough to no longer be considered a fish. In my case, the convicts knew that I wanted to learn their culture, and they wanted me to succeed so I could attain my goal of writing a book and telling it like it is. Consequently, they actively taught me how to see their culture in a cultural relativistic sense—without judging or condemning.

Let me explain *cultural relativism*—a concept that is paramount in anthropological research. It is based on the propositions that: each person's *value* system is learned; learned *value*s differ from one society to another; *value*s are related to the culture in which they occur; there are no universal *value*s, but we should respect the values of each of the world's cultures.

Using cultural relativism, I was able to understand what may appear to be strange or immoral or illegal behavior to outsiders. The principal underlying value of the Chicano prisoners' subculture is *machismo*. The behavior that Chicano prisoners exhibit in their subculture is based on this extremely important underlying value.

Another thing I did, as an anthropologist, while conducting my research was to consciously shed my *ethnocentrism*—the mixture of belief and feeling that one's own way of life is desirable and actually superior to others'.

It was interesting to note that the Chicanos respected *my* cultural background and never pushed me to do something that the larger US culture felt was unacceptable behavior—i.e illegal. In contrast, I cannot say the same for the actions of the FBI, other governmental agencies and individuals. They repeatedly tried to get me to do illegal things!

In the talks that I gave at universities, colleges, service organizations and Chicano groups, I developed an ability to successfully stress to the listeners that the prisoners were normal men—normal cultural animals—who should be treated with *human dignity* and respected for their cultural diversity. I was particularly surprised when I succeeded with groups such as the American Legion and the Southern California Probation, Parole and Correctional Society.

Change is persistent in a large, complex culture such as ours, where many subcultures are in contact with and often are in conflict with each other. I had hoped that if we understand a particular subculture, perhaps we could influence or control the course of that change.

Before Convict Unity Holiday, I was angry and outraged by what I had discovered. As a good red-blooded American adult with a strong sense of right and wrong, I had learned about an ideal prison system that was abused by some staff members at the expense of prisoners. A sense of treatment with human dignity often was missing. The Adult Authority, CDC and prison administrators perpetuated the charade of being able to determine when a prisoner is rehabilitated

Before and after Convict Unity Holiday, I understood the need for the FBI in a large, complex, free culture. However, I personally drew a line at and was outraged that the FBI, Prison administrators, or other governmental agencies continued trying to set me up or entice me to commit felonies, destroy my professional life and my family.

Applied anthropology—one of the sub-sections of anthropology— uses anthropological knowledge to influence social interaction, to maintain or change social institutions, or to direct the course of cultural change. One of my specialties in my doctoral studies was applied anthropology. I was taught to believe that in a complex society with many ways of life in contact with each other and often in conflict, change is persistent.

Some anthropologists think that it may be an illusion to think that people can *control* the course of change, or can modify the resulting cultural conflict. Others contend that if we can understand human cultures—including our own—the illusion may become reality.

I realize that, at times, the practice of applied anthropology can prove to be quite challenging. There are examples in the anthropological literature of both successes and failures.

In spite of my efforts over many years to bring about legitimate, legal changes in the less-than-ideal and often abusive California prison system, little underlying change has occurred.

Some people believe that prisons and other correctional institutions are the principal means by which our culture enforces conformity to the norms of our national culture. But this is not always true. Granted, for the vast majority in any culture, conformity results in the internalization of *value*s which we—in the larger national culture—learn and internalize through imitation, identification, and instruction. These desired values provide security and contribute to a sense of personal and cultural identity. Therefore, individuals cling to those *learned values*, and many feel threatened when confronted by others who live according to different ideas of what is desirable.

Now, consider the conflict that arises when Chicanos prisoners and the Mexican Mafia are added to the larger US cultural mix—not only in prison, but also on the streets. One of the *core values* of the Chicano subculture is *machismo*. Since a principle behavioral manifestation of *machismo* is the *refusal to snitch*, it has enabled Chicanos—from barrio neighborhood gangs on the streets to the depths of California prisons—to adapt and succeed.

Earlier in this memoir, I treated the endeavors of Chicanos in prisons and on the streets to address two major problems that many Chicanos face: poor language skills and poor or non-existent job training (BEMA class, EMPLEO). From numerous recent media reports, it appears that *some* Chicanos have adapted to the major issues of language skills and job training by *sidestepping* those problems.

By being *macho* and *refusing to snitch*, the Mexican Mafia has thrived, both in prisons and on the streets. Many young Chicanos in barrio street gangs look up to the Mexican Mafia and do what is asked of them by the Mexican Mafia. Even though reports indicate that the conflict between *La Eme* and *Nuestra Familia* factions still exist, the Mexican Mafia has gained even more control over the depths of the prisoner culture in California prisons. Also, reports indicate that the Mexican Mafia has established significant control over illegal drug trade in Chicano barrios through members of Chicano barrio neighborhood gangs.

Anthropology today is a science concerned with understanding how people can survive in a world where village, hamlet, city and nation are all *multicultural*. In isolation, each *value* system is interesting. *Crowded into close and intimate contact, these distinct culture patterns often lead to conflict, oppression and warfare.*

In my study of Chicano prisoners in San Quentin and beyond, I have observed the intensification of the conflict, oppression and virtual warfare between the **Chicano convict subculture** and the subculture of prison staff and administrators, and CDC officials which I will call the **CDC subculture**. Let me share the possible views of this conflict between these two opposing subcultures according to what might be their own perception.

The Chicano convicts perhaps proudly view their *macho* behavior leading to changes and increased power with pride. The *macho* core value of their subculture has served them well in their struggle against the CDC subculture. The Chicano convicts do recognize that they have not won—and may never win—their battle to eliminate the abuses they must endure from CDC; and, to a degree they have chosen to ignore the abuses which the California legislature should eliminate. However, they have increased their power and exercise control over many things inside and outside of prison that authorities—in spite of their efforts—have been unable to stop. From the Chicano convicts' perspective, they have reason to be proud of their accomplishments.

From the CDC side of the subcultural conflict, the efforts of CDC are focused in two main directions: elimination of the Mexican Mafia and its power inside California prisons, and preservation of the secrecy of CDC's abuses of the ideal prison system from the public.

CDC's many efforts to eliminate the Mexican Mafia have met with limited success. CDC—often with the assistance of the FBI, DEA and US Attorneys—has locked members of the Mexican Mafia up in Pelican Bay (the extremely secure and most remote prison in California); severely limited members' contact with the outside; tapped phone conversations; and used snitches, undercover agents and other things in its war against the Mexican Mafia. Prosecutions by local authorities generally have failed or been rather ineffective because local police officers usually have refused to testify against the Mexican Mafia, fearing execution by the Mexican Mafia. In contrast, Federal Prosecutions have been one of the only truly effective ways to fight the Mexican Mafia (as I treated earlier in "Mexican Mafia Trial"). However, even those successful prosecutions have done little to thwart the efforts and power of the Mexican Mafia, because the power of the Mexican Mafia is *not* pyramidal in shape as in the *Italian* Mafia—with a single leader at the top and less power as it goes to the wide base of the pyramid. In contrast, the *Mexican* Mafia is horizontally organized into many cells which all share power. This power structure is difficult for authorities to stop because conviction of a relatively small number of members on Federal RICO Act conspiracy charges and/or murder charges does not eliminate all of the many Mexican Mafia leaders.

Ideally CDC's war against the Mexican Mafia should succeed. However, I imagine that some who are engaged in that conflict on behalf of CDC feel that—even though they have learned a great deal about the Mexican Mafia over the years—their efforts have been less than successful.

In contrast, I imagine that members of the Mexican Mafia—even though they have lost some battles—take pride in the fact that they have not lost the war against CDC. Regardless of what tactics CDC uses, the Mexican Mafia has been able to adapt and expand its power.

Concerning CDC's secrecy regarding its abuses of the ideal prison system from the public, CDC appears to have succeeded. Little has been done in the last few years to inform the public of these abuses and it appears that significant changes through the legislature are not likely to soon occur. So, this battle appears to have been won by CDC.

However—even though the Mexican Mafia would like to see legitimate, lawful changes occur in the abusive actions by CDC in the prison system—the Mexican Mafia has chosen to successfully adapt to the existing abusive system. The Mexican Mafia takes pride in the fact that they are able to exercise their *machismo* and manipulate, thrive and grow in that abusive system.

To convey my own personal conclusions about this memoir and the things involved in my research among Chicanos prisoners is not a simple accomplishment for me. I have a plethora of mixed, often conflicting feelings—as an anthropologist, as a law-abiding member of the larger Anglo US culture, as an idealist who would like to see conflict in the world eliminated, and as a realist who recognizes that an ideal world free of conflict is not realistic.

As an anthropologist, I feel fortunate to have been helped by Chicano convicts to learn their subculture. I respect what they have been able to accomplish while living up to the principal core value of their subculture—*machismo*—while being imprisoned by the conflicting CDC subculture which represents an important part of the larger US culture. Chicano convicts are excellent representatives of how best to live up to the ideals of their subculture. With many, we became close, sincere friends.

As a law-abiding member of the larger Anglo US culture, I set aside my negative feelings about what the Chicano prisoners had previously done to result in their being incarcerated. I had to recognize that the Chicano prisoners were legally being punished for those offenses. As a law-abiding researcher, I conducted legitimate anthropological research into the depths of a subculture which was virtually hidden from outsiders. I have no regrets about succeeding in my unique research and writing a book that was in print and useful for 28 years to those—including legislators— who wanted to understand that obscure subculture. Personally, I do hope that my research and activities among and on behalf of Chicano prisoners since 1966 will—in some way—

produce positive changes that have yet to occur. However, my hope may be unrealistically optimistic.

I continue to be extremely disturbed by the actions of prison administrators, CDC, the FBI, and other governmental agencies and individuals. Were their actions predicated by the fact that my legitimate anthropological research was a threat to CDC? To me, their illegal and immoral actions conveyed a terrifying message: this is our country, and you could be next, even if you've done nothing wrong!

(By the way, while conducting my research among Chicano prisoners, I also learned about the guards' subculture, including the often unrealistic demands imposed on guards by that subculture. However, I did not attempt to include the guards' subculture in *Chicano Prisoners* because it was definitely extraneous to my study of Chicano prisoners.)

As an idealist, there were many things I would have changed—if possible. I would have converted the California prison system into a truly realistic and effective *correctional* system; one that is relevant to the larger culture on the streets, one that effectively prepares prisoners for their legal return into the world outside prison walls, where a decent job precludes the need to engage in illegal activities. I would have had California legislators institute legal changes in the prison system to eliminate the existing abusive practices and secrecy within CDC.

As a realist, I recognize that many of the things I would ideally change will probably never occur, and it is probably naive of me to think those things could easily be changed. It is seldom possible to arbitrarily change subcultures and cultures so they no longer are in conflict with each other. To change a prison system into an *ideal* correctional system is unrealistic; most prisoners are too busy learning and surviving in the prisoner culture to be bothered about most rehabilitative activities; and most guards are too involved with enforcing the demands required of them to be concerned with activities they consider extraneous to maintaining order.

About thirty years ago, I recognized through feedback from a few staff members that CDC was quite upset by the increasing violence and number of deaths that were occurring behind the walls of California prisons. The resulting negative publicity was embarrassing for officials who ideally were in charge of the prisoners and should be able to minimize violent activities.

Staff efforts to thwart violent and often deadly prisoner activity—particularly by the Mexican Mafia—over the ensuing years have done little to stop the alarming increase in violence and deaths. The Mexican Mafia has become deadlier, more powerful and quite adept at side-stepping staff efforts to control them. At times, the efforts by staff to control the Mexican Mafia have resulted in much less success than have the efforts by the Mexican Mafia to control so much activity inside California prisons as well as illegal activities on the streets.

I personally contend that—from top CDC officials and administrators down to the guards—they have been too busy fighting to control the Mexican Mafia to devote time to revamping the California prison system. I recognize that guards face a nearly impossible challenge. Unfortunately for them, I can't imagine how they will succeed.

Let me word things differently. Let me temporarily expand the meaning of both of the conflicting subcultures treated above. Think of the Chicano convict subculture as the "*Mexican Mafia/Chicano convict, barrio street gang subculture.*" Also, think of the CDC subculture as the "*CDC/law enforcement subculture.*" The conflict between these subcultures is great and deep-seated. Very deep cultural forces are involved in both sides of that conflict.

Initially the Mexican Mafia and Chicano convicts were quite concerned about the problems faced by Chicanos in the areas of job training and language skills. However, when efforts to bring about legitimate changes years ago failed to bring about results, they realistically seemed to *sidestep* those issues by substituting their focus on expanding their power inside prison and on the streets.

Now the Mexican Mafia, with its recently-increased power, controls even more of the prisoner's subcultural depths inside prison and most of the drug traffic in the barrios as well as in California prisons. With this new power, the Mexican Mafia and Chicanos no longer need the previously-desired education and job skills training. They now are able to make money while using the barrio language they have already learned without formal job or educational training. For the Mexican Mafia side of the subcultural conflict, most of their *macho* efforts have been successful, something to be proud of. The Mexican Mafia may have lost a couple of *battles* to federal prosecutors, but the Mexican Mafia still appears to be winning the *war*.

The principal efforts of the CDC/law enforcement subculture has been to imprison, control and prevent illegal in-prison activities of prisoners and some Mexican Mafia activities on the streets. True, there are very few escapes from prison, and efforts by CDC to preserve CDC's secrecy from the public have been largely successful. In addition, federal prosecutions of some Mexican Mafia members have been successful; but, as I earlier noted, these prosecutions have done little to diminish the power and influence of the Mexican Mafia—both inside prison and on the streets. So, it appears that the CDC side in the war is winning, but those wins are merely *battles* in its *war* against the Mexican Mafia.

The major conflict in the war between CDC and the Mexican Mafia is about the increasing power of the Mexican Mafia—which CDC has been unable to stop. As noted before, federal prosecutions have been successful, but that limited success is far removed from actually winning the war. Even though CDC has developed new tools in its attempt to control the Mexican Mafia, those new tools have had little impact on the obvious success of the Mexican Mafia which appears to be winning the war at this time.

My Deep-Rooted Personal Feelings

Let me share a few of my firmly established sentiments about anthropology as a discipline from the early 1960's and the Cold War era to the present. My feelings are based on events involved in anthropological research throughout the world during those tumultuous years as well as my own research among Chicano prisoners during part of that time. What I feel about my own research and some of the consequences of conducting research when and where I did is not unrelated from what was happening to many other anthropologists and their research and activities throughout the world—as well as the upheavals in American anthropology as a discipline.

From the beginning of my undergraduate student days, I have long-recognized that anthropology is an extremely ethical discipline. When an anthropologist studies "natives," regardless of where they are found in the world, the anthropologist establishes a relationship of *trust* with those natives. Not unlike the pledge of doctors, anthropologists explicitly or implicitly pledge to **do no harm to the natives being studied.** Chicano prisoners and I had that type of mutual, deep-felt personal trust.

During the Cold War and into the Vietnam War era, Don Faville—a dear friend of mine from Junior High School days on—was an anthropology graduate student at U.C. Berkeley when I returned from two years of service in the US Army. Don was in the doctoral program, fluently spoke Chinese, and his geographical area of specialty was China and Southeast Asia.

Soon, having completed his doctoral exams, he was ready to go to Southeast Asia to do research which would become the basis for his doctoral dissertation. Unfortunately, Don's application for research funds failed—he would have to wait a year to apply again. However, he didn't want to merely hang around Berkeley for a year, so he took a two-year job in Burma. I—as well as other friends of his—asked Don who he was working for. He would not directly answer. However, he went on to explain that while he was doing his job, he would be able to gather enough information to enable him to return to Berkeley and write his dissertation from that material. Regardless of how many times he was asked—even explicitly if it was the CIA he would be working for—he would *always* give the identical reply. "I'm working for a very high level, secret interdepartmental agency."

Don did indicate that he would be working with Burmese peasants in their villages and would write reports about the kinship and social structure of those villagers. Those reports would be delivered to his employer. At that time, on the surface, this basic anthropological research sounded innocuous to those of us who questioned the nature of his research—even though he still refused to admit that he was working for the CIA. Don, in an extremely private conversation with me, revealed that he truly believed his rather isolated research in a few peasant villages could not really be considered spying.

After Don had been in Burma for over a year, he had a bit of a misunderstanding with his fiancée. It soon was resolved, and all was well again. Then Don's parents were notified that he was dead! Supposedly, two days after writing his last letter to his fiancée—when he was well—he developed a massive kidney infection, was helicoptered out to Bangkok and died! There were no mortuary facilities available, so when his body arrived in the US it was in very bad shape. His parents could not bear to identify his body, so a close friend identified his decomposed body.

Based on other similar things we had heard about the untimely or questionable deaths of other anthropologists in Southeast Asia, many of us at Berkeley concluded that he probably was shot to death by one side or the other in the internal conflict in Burma. We felt it was quite *unlikely* that he had developed and died of a massive kidney infection in two days!

Among anthropologists, there were strong negative feelings about the CIA and research in Southeast Asia—as well as other places in the world at that time. CIA agents had found it convenient to use anthropology as a cover for its spying activities. The *obvious, observable* activities of a CIA agent and an anthropologist were not too different— both did not have a job and merely walked about or hung around asking questions and taking notes. This deception by the CIA, coupled with hiring anthropologists like Don to actually spy for the CIA, infuriated most, but not all anthropologists.

At one of the annual meetings of the American Anthropological Association, a young anthropologist tried to bring this issue up at the huge semi-formal dinner/meeting for all members. The older, conservative chairperson refused to recognize the young anthropologist who was waving her hand to be recognized. Frustrated, the young anthropology graduate student finally took off her shoes, stood on the white tablecloth-covered table and yelled at the chairperson to be heard about ethical issues in anthropology. She was heard!

Within months a four- or five-person Ethics Committee was formed to look into the abuse of anthropologists and their research by the CIA. Margaret Mead was the Chairperson, and Professor Dave Olmsted, the chairman of my doctoral committee at U.C. Davis, was one of the members. The committee's activities delved deeply into the issues involved.

By the way, in a year or two, the young graduate student—who had stood on the table and yelled at the chairperson and was heard—had her PhD and was elected to become the new President of the American Anthropological Association.

One of many upsetting discoveries by the Ethics Committee was that Don and other young anthropologists had been deceived by the CIA. The research of each young anthropologist alone *did* seem innocuous. However, when the seemingly legitimate research results of *several* young anthropologists who were conducting research in different peasant villages in the same country (Burma for example) were combined, the CIA was able to determine the kinship, tribal or other social relationships of individuals—including which individuals were the most powerful. This information was then used by the CIA and others in covert counterinsurgency activities—activities that often were detrimental to the peasants with whom the individual young anthropologists had supposedly established mutual trust.

When I protested the war in Vietnam while at Cabrillo College, I did so because of what I had learned about peasantry as a societal type. Usually peasants are the losers when there is war or revolution in a predominantly peasant country. I must admit my compassion for the peasants, whether they are in Mexico, Guatemala, Vietnam or elsewhere.

When two opposing groups are fighting for control of a peasant country, the peasants are almost always the losers. If the peasants, under threat of harm or death, support side A, they are seen as the enemy of side B and treated as such by side B. Then, at another time, when under the threat of harm or death by side B, the peasants support side B, and side A sees them as the enemy. They are forced to support the side that is threatening them at that moment. However, the peasants have little understanding of the politics and power in the larger country and often have no deep feelings of support for either side in the war for control of the country. The peasants almost always have been and will be abused by those who exercise economic and political control over them. In times of conflict or revolution to change the leadership of their country, the peasants usually are the losers. ***Regardless of which side wins, the same type of individuals take control of the country and exercise the same type of control over the peasants.*** Setting cunning political rhetoric aside, realistically, the life and culture of the peasants does not significantly change.

Let me verbally share a picture that appeared in the Watsonville paper during the Vietnam war. An elderly Vietnamese man was walking behind a water buffalo, plowing his huge rice paddy with a single-bladed wooden plow. In the middle of the rice paddy was a giant crater from a huge bomb. It was obvious from the picture that each time the man came to the crater he had to go around it. The caption below the picture translated and quoted the peasant who simply said, "I wish they would leave me alone so I could grow my rice."

The details of warfare or revolt in a peasant country may vary from country to country, but some things are constants—death of peasant men, women and children; and destruction of their homes and villages. However, regardless of the outcome and the winner, one thing seldom changes: the peasants are always the losers!

I do feel that my protest of the war in Vietnam was justified and legitimate. For administrators at Cabrillo College to use my protest against the Vietnamese War and my legitimate criticism of CDC, as the *unspoken real* reasons for firing me is a sad commentary on the many conflicting aspects found in the larger US culture.

Personally, I believe that *DANGER AND TRUST: SAN QUENTIN, THE MEXICAN MAFIA AND THE CHICANO MOVEMENT*, the title of this memoir, is quite appropriate. I openly admit that my many years of involvement have been many things: exciting, frustrating, frightening and rewarding. Thanks for letting me share this memoir with you.